SIR TOM JONES: 80

The early days and the incredible rise of the young Tommy Woodward

Colin MacFarlane

DEDICATED TO THE REAL SIR TOM JONES CAST –
Vernon Hopkins, Gordon Mills, Alan Woodward, Johnny Bennett, Dai Perry, Brian Blackler, Micky Gee, Geoffrey Bloomer, Myron and Byron, Keith Davies, Joan Lister, Tommy Pitman, and all the former members of the Wood Road Non Political Club.

Many thanks also Cardiff Library staff, Abdul, Hannah and Sarah.

Tom: 80 Head of Production, Norman Faulkner. Production team Philippa MacFarlane, Helen John and Mark Stentiford, Cardiff Print Centre.

'To be born in Wales is not to be born with a silver spoon in your mouth, it is to be born with music in your heart and poetry in your soul.'

To Colin-Peter, Liz and Ross   -
we all grew up together.

CONTENTS

TOM JONES 80. PROLOGUE

Sir Tom Jones 80 on June 7 2020 – who would have believed it? Over the course of more than 50 years he has had an amazing career – meeting the likes of Presley and Sinatra and knighted along the way. But uncannily he has outlived them all. Sadly his wife Linda, died in 2016 and it must have deeply affected him. They had been together since teenagers – a love affair that lasted a lifetime. Tom is still popular all over the world with disco hits like Kiss and Sex Bomb pounding out.

The Green, Green Grass of Home and Delilah are now considered Welsh national anthems. Now he is mainly known by a younger generation as a judge on The Voice. But that is only the tip of the iceberg. If only they knew the full story of how Tommy Woodward from Treforest had an incredible rise to fame.

This book is primarily about his early days until the song The Boy from Nowhere in 1987. Author Colin MacFarlane was lucky enough to interview the main characters of the real Tom Jones Show back in the 1980s before they all departed. Sir Tom can't believe he is 80 and still has and eye for the grannies who fancy him. You can't teach an old dog new tricks!

Age will not wither him, the songs and his legend will live forever.

THE STORY BEHIND THE BOOK

It was a bizarre scenario. After leaving college I had come all the way from Scotland and found myself working as a junior reporter in Tom's home town of Pontypridd. While working on the Pontypridd Observer I lived in Tom's village of Treforest. After work I would have a few pints in some of the local pubs and found that everyone had a Tom Jones' story. I eventually ended up hanging about the Wood Road Non Political Club just a few yards from my house.

Tom's family, the Woodwards, had a long history of drinking there. His father and uncles had all frequented the place over the years and for them it was a home from home. It really was a goldmine of local stories, not only about Tom, but about local characters who were ideal news material for this small town valley's paper. Sitting in the club, night after night, surrounded by these hard drinking men, I got to know the real cast of the Tom Jones Show. It was 1982 and Tom had long hit the road to stardom in 1965 with It's Not Unusual. But 17 years later the cast were still there knocking back pints and carrying on with their lives as they had always done.

The real Tom Jones Show cast.
Dai Perry. Now Dai was an interesting character, a hard beer guzzling stocky man who looked like an ex rugby player, He was rough, tough and hard to bluff. He was Tom's lifelong best pal and later bodyguard, but after punching a photographer when on tour of Venezuela in 1974 he was unceremoniously sacked by Gordon Mills. Dai found himself back in Treforest with not a lot of money but was rich in Tom Jones' stories. While having a pint with him, some of the stories of him being with Tom and Elvis were so incredible I suggested we write a book together. Under the influence of much beer, Dai readily agreed. But he had a reputation as a mercurial character and could change his mind as quick as the weather. One night he was boasting about being with Tom and Elvis and a particularly drunk guy disputed it all saying Dai was talking bullshit. Dai was advised not to hit him. The drunk guy challenged Dai to bring in pics with him Tom and Elvis, to prove his stories were true. The next night we all waited in the club with great expectations, but no sign of Dai. Someone said, "It was all baloney. I bet he never met Elvis!" But the next night Dai entered the club armed with a portfolio of photos. There it was in hard photographic evidence, Tom, Elvis and Dai, that soon shut up the inebriated doubters.

A while later I brought out the original version of this book, *The Boy from Nowhere.* I was walking along Wood Road about 11.15 pm when I heard an aggressive drunken shout, "Hey, you put me in that effing book!" I was Dai swaying his arms in my direction. He chased me but I made off hiding in a dark alleyway to avoid his wrath. The next day Tom's cousin, Alan Woodward, intervened and Dai was given a copy of the book. A further meeting ensued and this time Dai was like a big pussycat, saying everything was all right, he was slightly pleased to have been mentioned in the story of Tom's life. I met him on another occasion in the Globe pub on the nearby Graig. I asked him what Elvis was really like. He took a sip of his pint and said, "Elvis? He was a boring bastard!" A few years later Dai had a heart operation and afterwards he could be seen jogging around the hills near Treforest. Tragically he died of a heart attack while on the Welsh hills.

Alan Woodward. Alan was arguably Tom's closest cousin and was proud of his incredible achievements. He would tell me stories over a pint that could not be written about at the time for legal reasons. He had quite a few cracking yarns to tell. When he was laid off from his job with a redundancy payment, he phoned Tom and was invited over to join him in Beverly Hills. When on the plane he met two elderly ladies who asked him where he was going. He told them he was flying to L.A. to see his cousin. One of them asked, "Who is your cousin?"
"Tom Jones."
"What *the* Tom Jones?
"Aye!"
When Alan got off the plane, the two nosy women followed him out of the airport. Suddenly a Rolls Royce pulled up with TJ number plate on the front. Alan climbed in and gave the nosy ladies a wave

goodbye. Later that night Alan was in Tom's mansion playing pool and drinking "At least a £1,000 worth of champagne." When he asked Tom what it was like making love to Miss World, Tom replied, "It was like jumping into the deep end of a swimming pool." Tom's birthday was coming up and Alan asked him what he could buy for his birthday. Tom laughed and said, "A new knob!" The following day they flew by private jet to Las Vegas. At a party in a hotel Alan was approached by a beautiful statuesque blonde. She was all over him. But Tom whispered in his ear that it was in fact a man. They could not stop laughing later when a drunk record executive got off with the blonde and headed to his hotel suite with her.

During the trip Alan hung around with Hollywood celebrities like Gene Hackman and had a pic taken with him. When he came back it hung proudly on his terraced house living room wall. A few years later Alan died of a brain haemorrhage while still in his early 60s.

Brian Blackler, Keith Davies, Joan Lister, Geoffrey Bloomer. Through Alan I met fellow club member Brian Blackler who had brilliant stories about growing up with Tom, including going on holiday with him. Guitarist Keith Davies was another gem of a find and had amazing tales about the beginning of Tom's early career starting at an audition in a Rhydyfelin council house. Former landlady of the Wheatsheaf pub Joan Lister lived not far from the club in what looked like a mansion. She had great clarity about how the young Tommy Woodward changed the atmosphere of the pub with his voice. "When Tom sang nobody talked, they just listened in amazement," she recalled. I got to know Geoffrey Bloomer over the years in Pontypridd. An educated man who liked a drink too many but a brilliant character. He has a significant mention in Tom's autobiography as Geoffrey taught him how to drive while they were trying to punt Hoovers around the houses. Geoffrey even showed me a novel he had written called *Vengeance is mine sayeth Morgan* and had an initial publishing contract as well. But it never made it to print. Ironically when I met him over the years he never mentioned his connection to Tom. He is no longer around but is still remembered as a great character.

Johnny Bennett. Johnny was an important player in the real Tom Jones Show. He had been big pals with Gordon Mills in Trealaw and was even instrumental in introducing Gordon to Tom. In many way he had a hang up about Tom's success. Johnny was also reckoned to be a good singer around the clubs but never made it. He showed me a small red diary he had kept from the early days which including the first night Gordon met Tom at the Lewis Merthyr Club in Porth. Years later when Tom became a big star, Johnny phoned up Gordon and said he had heard a brilliant singer "Who is it?" Gordon asked.

"A guy called Tony Christie"

"Is he as good as Tom?"

"Better" Johnny replied.

Gordon hung up the phone and never talked to him again.

When I talked to Johnny several years later he was crestfallen, he had lost his precious little diary which had detailed outlines of the early days of Tom Jones. It would have been worth a fortune in today's memorabilia auction world.

Tommy Pitman. He was the guy that Tom replaced in the Senators. The regulars in the Wood Road Club reckoned he had a good voice, as good as Tom's, but it was always debateable. The argument was Tommy never made it because he never got the lucky breaks, like Tom meeting Gordon etc. Tommy was a quiet unassuming guy, who at the time in the Senators loved playing cards. This led to his downfall when he failed to appear at a gig at Ponty YMCA and Tom was persuaded to take over the mic. I often played against him at football, a kick about at the local park in Treforest, but never bothered to ask him any Tom Jones' stories as I could tell years later he was still affected by Tom's rapid rise to international fame. He lived the rest of his of his life in a terraced house not far from where Tom was brought up.

Vernon Hopkins. Probably the most important player in the early days of the real Tom Jones Show. He spotted Tom and got him in his band The Senators. But years later Tom bombed him out. He has written a brilliant book called Just Help Yourself describing the antics of the young Tom when he was in the band and they moved to London. There is a touch of bitterness about his book, but a great tale. Vernon said in an interview, "The book is a recording of history: the story of what happened in the 60s, the rise to stardom and what happened to the band. And what happened is that we got betrayed, so to speak. It's a 400 -page moralistic story of how the music industry worked in the 60s, when it was a cut-throat business. It still is, but even more so back then".

"The book is about the lack of loyalty as far as Tom Jones and his manager were concerned. When *It's Not Unusual* came out, things changed. It's about Tom Jones but not who he is, *what* he is. It's different, what the fans see and what person he is behind the curtain. I got behind the curtain and I know exactly what happened. What celebrities put forward is an image, so of course the fans like them. But behind that they're people and we're all characters. Some are nice characters and some are nasty characters. And then there's the title, which has a double meaning. One is the title of the 1968 song, called *Help Yourself*. But also, all he ever did after *It's Not Unusual* was just help himself. Not only when it came to the band, with other people as well. The reader can decide what title they prefer – *Just Help Yourself* as the title of the song or as a description of what happened."

Gordon Mills. Back working at the Ponty Observer, the editor Jim Campbell called me in and said he had fixed up interviews with Gordon and Tom over the phone from L.A. Obviously this was a big scoop and he handed me the job. I went to the office at 11pm and first talked to Gordon on the phone. He said he often got fed up with the USA showbiz life and yearned for a pint in his local club in Trealaw, Tonypandy, where he had been brought up. It was 1983, the eve of Tom's first tour of the UK in a decade. This was a big occasion for me as I had been used to covering golden weddings and the local magistrate court. Now I was in deep conversation with arguably the top music manager in the world! During the course of the conversation I could sense Gordon was playing a cat and mouse game with me. Finally he seemed to relent and said, "Do you want a world exclusive?"

A world exclusive for a junior reporter like me at the Ponty Observer! "Well I've never told anyone this before but Elvis asked me to manage him."

Me: (gulp) "What Elvis asked you to be his manager? What about Col Tom Parker?"

"Elvis was fed up with him so he wanted me to take over. Can you imagine that? A bus conductor from Tonypandy managing the King?"

I was flabbergasted. Too flabbergasted to write the story so it never went in to print. It was not a Ponty Observer story – more suited to the Hollywood Reporter, the LA Times or National Enquirer.

Three years later in 1986 Gordon, a heavy smoker, died of cancer in an L.A. hospital at the age of 51. He was arguably the greatest pop manager of his time – moulding the careers of Tom Jones, Engelbert Humperdinck, Gilbert O' Sullivan and many more. What a brilliant book he could have written – if he had more time on the Earth.

Tom Jones. After the phone conversation with Gordon I talked to Tom himself. I had met all the main cast characters and now I had the chance to converse with the main character. It was an easy going conversation. Tom said when he got back home he would be meeting up with all his pals at the Wood Road Club – many of whom I now considered friends. Ironically he sounded like fame had not changed him. I could imagine if he had not made it he would have ended up sitting in the club with Alan, Dai and the rest of the boys. A few years later on the verge of launching my book The Boy from Nowhere in 1988 I had a night out in Cardiff with a pal, Mark Horton. We went into Cardiff's Marriott Hotel and lo and behold Tom was standing at the bar with his son and manager Mark Woodward. Horton told them I was writing a Tom Jones' biography and they both came over and shook my hand. A surreal moment.

When the book came out a guy approached me and Alan in local club with a recording on a video camera. It had Tom Jones on stage at Las Vegas. A woman was standing at the front of the stage holding my book asking him to sign it. Tom said, "I can remember a Scottish guy telling me he was writing a book on me. Are there any dirty bits in it?" The woman shook her head.

Tom replied, "Well he doesn't know me that well, does he?" It was the end of an odyssey being involved in the real Tom Jones Show with all its real cast members.

Original Acknowledgements

I first got the idea for this book back in 1983. While working as a reporter on a local newspaper I interviewed Tom Jones and Gordon Mills by phone from America before the first major tour for ten years .I found Tom Jones to be an extremely down to earth chap who seemed a trifle homesick. The things he told me during our conversation merely reinforced all the stories I had heard about him while living in his home village of Treforest, Pontypridd.

Later, at a press conference in Newport, I got the chance to talk to him again but what surprised me was how ignorant other journalists seemed to be of the Tom Jones story. Of course, I had the unfair advantage of living in the same area as Tom's family and friends. Some of these people also became my friends and I was constantly asked 'If you say you are a writer, why not do a book on Tom?' When I talked to Gordon Mills at length for a second time I told him of my idea and he said: 'OK, don't talk about it, do it.'

Gordon recounted to me those early days when he had the bravado and nothing else. But his bravado was behind Tom all the way and in the end it paid off. It was not until early 1986 1 actually began to write this book with Gordon's words ringing in my ears. At times it proved to be an uphill task trying to construct Tom's early years. Some people were only too pleased to talk, others you could feel kept things back, and others refused to say anything at all. But these people were in the minority. All in all, I interviewed more than 100 people, including Tom and Gordon, and researched more than 30,000 press cuttings from all over the world to build up an accurate picture of the man's life story over the years.

Indeed, I would imagine there are things in this book that even Tom will have forgotten and perhaps when he becomes old and tired he will look at his life through the pages of this book and say: 'What a great bloody life I have had.'

During the course of interviewing people it was Tom's first cousin, and spokesman for the family, Alan Woodward, from Tower Street, Treforest, who managed to open doors for me. He would reassure the reluctant that it was all right to speak to me and he would encourage the eager to re-tell favourite stories of the young Tom. At times he stayed in the background as I interviewed many people but his voice could always be heard if he thought the person concerned was not telling the true or complete story. Alan was with me from the start and shared the good times and bad times during the writing of this book. Sometimes we would get so disillusioned we would make for a pub and drown our sorrows. At other times we felt so elated we would head for the same pub and celebrate loudly, with Tom's music playing in the background. We spent one of the best nights ever at Johnny Bennett's house in Trealaw, Tonypandy. Johnny was brought up with Gordon Mills and proved to be a unique fund of information who could remember exact times, dates and whole conversations with Tom and Gordon which had never before been placed on the record. Another great day was spent at Leslie Lawrie's house in Solihull, Birmingham. Leslie is the president of the Tom Jones Rhondda Boy Fan Club and to say her house is a shrine to Tom would not be an exaggeration. It was she who gave us the fan's perspective on Tom.

It was she who had searched the libraries and bookshops for years looking for a book on Tom. It was she who gave me her collection of more than 30,000 press cuttings from all over the world dating back to 1964.Without these three people the book could not have been written properly. Finally I would like to pay my gratitude to all those I interviewed and who were kind enough to give me their time and part of their lives to reveal the truth about the "Boy from Nowhere".

Introduction

The lights dim. The hall is silent except for a few gasps which punctuate the stillness. It's like waiting for a bomb to go off. The silence is broken, a voice says 'And here he is. Tom Jones.' A spotlight hits the centre stage and to the strains of 'It's Not Unusual' the man they have all been waiting for bounds onto the stage. He is a middle-aged man with short black hair, a dark suit and an open-necked shirt with a crucifix shining from his hairy chest. He has a gleam in his eye and a sexual, predatory look on his face. But it is his torso that commands your immediate attention. It moves rather erratically to and fro. It is as if this middle-aged man is a dog on heat. It is as if this man, who has been happily married for more than thirty years, is trying to make love to every single female in the audience. Women who we might call 'aunty' or 'granny' — gasp and groan at the sight of this mythical sex-machine. For some of these women the excitement becomes too much. At first you notice their expensive hair do's bobbing in the air and then they rise, straightening out the creases in their skirts, before rushing towards the stage as if possessed by some demon. To the uninitiated what happens next comes as a bit of a shock. One lady — let's call her 'Granny' — aged about sixty, stands panting and drooling at the foot of the stage Granny's eyes are fixed firmly on Tom's torso. Her eyes have the glassy look of someone who has discovered a hidden treasure.

For that moment in time Granny is not normal. 'But,' you ask yourself 'what on earth is she going to do next?'

In a trance, Granny whips her hand under her skirt, takes her knickers off, and then throws them up on the stage at Tom's feet.

Tom picks them up and examines them closely. 'You're a big girl, aren't you?' he says. He then wipes his sweaty forehead with them and throws them back to Granny.

Clutching her knickers, now soaked with Tom Jones's sweat, Granny runs back to her seat, sobbing with pleasure fully satisfied.

This is sex in pantomime.

This is Tom Jones.

To the men in the audience Tom Jones is a parody, a caricature of what a real man should be. And what man can honestly say that he would not want the sex appeal of Jones?

But if one dismisses the blatant sexuality of the act what is one left with? The Voice, of course.

Over the years I have heard the Jones voice on numerous recordings but that is nothing compared to hearing him sing live. It is only then one can really appreciate the greatness of his talent.

To hear him sing 'I'm Coming Home' live is to feel something deeply emotional stir inside. As his voice rises powerfully from the stage and then reaches a crescendo, it seems to have a hypnotic effect on the mind.

The Jones act is a mixture of pure talent and pure sexuality. That is why he has been a star for more than twenty years and that is why he will continue.

To many, his appeal is ageless and timeless. And when you strip away the glitz and glamour around the man, at heart you will find that the boy from the valleys is still there. A boy who conquered the world with his voice.

1. The Boy from Nowhere

In bars and clubs all over South Wales drunks can be heard boasting about knowing the young Tom Jones. Clichés such as 'He was a right tearaway' and 'He still owes me the ten bob I lent him' can be heard spilling from their inebriated mouths. But if one actually bothers to ask them the real story behind Tom Jones's success they become muddled and the stories are full of contradictions and mistakes, based largely on barroom myth. Such is the price of success for a man who left his native environment more than twenty years ago to become an international star and multimillionaire who now lives in California.

The Tom Jones story is far more complex than the simple utterings of a boastful drunk; it is a complicated conglomeration of details and events, which, when carefully looked at, seems like one big magical jigsaw with thousands of different interlocking pieces.

Like Jolson and Presley, Tom Jones came from an underprivileged, poverty-ridden background; a certain course of lucky events shoved him into the limelight and carried him on a wave of success which even he himself finds hard to comprehend. Jones was similar to Jolson and Presley in more than one sense; he had a talent that impressed people, especially females, to an extent that they worshipped and adored him. It is a common part of human nature that people will admire those who have the rather superficial talent of performing successfully in front of them, and in the South Wales valleys such a talent is the rule rather than the exception.

Of course, there are performers and there are performers. There are those who will sing in public houses, clubs and bars even though they have no talent at all. They persist in their mediocrity until the audience becomes so disillusioned they begin booing or even worse…silence.

Jones, like Jolson and Presley, never had such problems because he had talent with a capital T. The way he sang and the way he moved his body to stimulate his rampant women fans, was in its own time highly original. Thomas John Woodward was born in the village of Treforest, near Pontypridd, Mid Glamorgan on 7 June 1940. Treforest is a small mining village that has seen better days, twelve miles from Cardiff. If you travel by the Rhondda Valley railway line it takes twenty-five minutes to get to from Cardiff Central Station. And what do you see when you get off the train? Row upon row, upon row, of terraced houses. Houses in which generations of people have been born, brought up, got married and eventually expired. Even to this day the whole sub-culture of the area relates back to the industrial revolution. More than 150 years ago a growing band of capitalists realized coal was the fuel that would keep the wheels of the industrial revolution turning, and in South Wales there was an abundance of this fuel.

Until the early nineteenth century Treforest was, as its name suggests, a large forest whose trees had stood undisturbed for centuries. There were swamps and an abundance of wildlife with a few farms and homesteads dotted around the area. The great oaks that grew in Treforest became the first victims of the industrial revolution. They were considered ideal for the building of ships and before 1805 thousands of trees were cut down for Nelson's fleet.

Later the Treforest Tin-plate Works and Treforest Iron Works sprang up and cut down the trees to use as fuel. In no time at all Treforest, and its main road, Wood Road, became stripped of all its trees. In nearby Pontypridd, coal seams were begging to be exploited and these seams stretched right up to the top of the Rhondda Valley. Coal was the black gold of the day and the gold rush, dirty and grimy as it was, took off.

People from all over the kingdom chanced their luck and headed for South Wales. Largely it was the luckless poor, the people who found it hard to feed their families and exist in other parts of Britain. New faces and new accents flooded into the area with families that cried out for a job, a wage and somewhere to live. They came with great expectations from Scotland, Ireland, and all parts of England and Wales. Many were to be disappointed but some were content with the new life they had found under the black god, coal. Jobs were in abundance in the mining industry for a wide variety of people whether they were miners, managers or clerks. Related industries also took off. Building, haulage, iron, steel, and eventually the railways provided even more jobs which made South Wales one of the most, if not the most, economically progressive areas in the country.

The tram road, and later the railway line, made Treforest a bustling centre of industry and commerce second only to the town of Merthyr Tydfil in its magnitude. Week by week thousands of people poured into Pontypridd and the Rhondda Valley. But there was a problem. The workers had to be accommodated, so from one end of the valley to the other end terraced houses were built. They were built on top of hills, at the bottom of hills, near mines and factories, anywhere where there was space available. With the oncoming of the industrial revolution a new sub-culture formed. It was, in a sense, a unique style of forced socialism. In Treforest everyone lived in much the same style house, got paid the same wage, shopped in the same shops and drank in the same hostelries. Everyone was considered equal and in the same boat, and if anyone tried to put on airs they would be shunned and mocked by the community.

There was only one thing these people admired, and that was talent. If you could sing you were appreciated by a hard-working and hard drinking population who saw you as an asset to their everyday life. It was into this cultural vacuum that Thomas John Woodward was destined to be born. Attitudes and actions had been formed during the coal boom and are still there today. Although Treforest is only twelve miles from Cardiff it is like a little world of its own, with its own characters and idiosyncrasies which in real terms have not changed dramatically since the industrial revolution. According to the relatives I talked to,Tom John Woodward's ancestors arrived from Cornwall during the industrial revolution. Over the generations every male member of the Woodward family made it his life to serve the industry of coal mining. Tom's grandfather was a miner, his father Tom Woodward was a miner and so were his uncles Edwin and George. For forty years Tom's father rose at 5.15 a.m. winter and summer to graft down the pit at the nearby Cwm Colliery, Beddau. He was proud of his mining heritage. After he retired he said, 'I was a pick-and-shovel man. Right up until I retired I brought up 14 tons of coal a day from the pit. That's how I worked, getting paid for how much I brought up per for per square yard. I never worked for a labourer's wage.'

Like many mining families, the Woodwards suffered through the bad times. Years after the 1926 General Strike Tom's father would recall how men, women and children would be starving in Treforest and have to queue up at soup kitchens because they had nothing to put in their bellies. But like other mining families, the Woodwards rode the storm and there were good times amid the hard work and everyday struggle for survival. They call Wales the Land of Song, and maybe that's because people were inclined to sing to alleviate their worries. The chapels encouraged it. The pubs and clubs encouraged it. So why not do it if you had the talent and could make people happy by singing? Out of the three Woodward brothers it was Edwin and George who emerged as the singers of the family. They were always in demand for a song in the clubs, pubs, weddings, parties, or any other celebrations that were going on in the Treforest community. Tom's father was not in the same singing league but would sing if asked to, but that was rarely. Like all ordinary working class men in Treforest he liked dancing, a few pints at the weekends and a bet on the horses.

It was at one of the local dancehalls he met Freda Jones in 1933. They were soon married and moved in with Freda's family at 57 Kingsland Terrace, Treforest. In 1934 their first child was born, a daughter, Sheila. The couple yearned for a son and eventually their dream came true six years later when on 7 June 1940 Tom was born at 57, Kingsland Terrace. The birth was registered at Pontypridd Register Office on 1 July 1940 and witnessed by registrar Gwilym James. There was no hesitation about naming him — he was to be called exactly the same as his father, Thomas John Woodward. On the birth certificate Tom's father put down his occupation as 'Assistant Colliery Repairer (below ground)'. The family were delighted with the arrival of the baby boy, the heir to the mining throne, who according to his mother 'slept like a dream' and rarely disturbed his parents during the night. It was as though Tom had been a gift from God. A light that suddenly brightened up their lives. Soon Tom Senior, mother Freda, and sister Sheila began to notice something unusual about him. At the age of six months he began to make noises 'like musical notes' and would react violently if anyone dared to stop his performance. Freda in turn would sing to him and that seemed to keep him quiet. Even in those early days the family began to realize that there was nothing the Woodward boy liked better than a good song. In addition to this raw untapped talent he had another thing going for him — good looks. Neighbours would remark to Freda that he was an outstandingly handsome baby as he had a mass of blond curly hair that tended to make other mothers envious.

The Woodward boy was not without his problems though. He was rather overweight and as time passed by his family feared he might have difficulty walking. He could crawl all right but seemed too lazy to walk. The family had always been good at improvising and soon Tom was encouraged to chase his sister Sheila with a stick. At first there was little response. But after a few weeks he managed to find his feet and one day, much to the delight of his family, ran after Sheila around the kitchen table.

During Tom's early childhood his grandfather died and so the family moved to the old Woodward home at 44 Laura Street, Treforest. In a way they were relieved; it was a bigger house than Kingsland Terrace, three storeys, and had more space for the growing boy and his sister.

The extra space also gave Tom an early chance to develop his talent. Tom recalled his early childhood days: 'My mother says I could sing before I could walk and that I would crawl about the floor giving voice for all I was worth. She used to treat it as a joke until one day I was singing a song I had picked up from the radio and she stopped what she was doing. "Sing that again," she said. It was called "Mairzy Doats and Dozy Doats". I sang it and she said, "You know, you've got a lovely voice." I was five and after that there was no stopping me.'

Soon all the family could see that the Woodward boy had something special, something unique, and it was encouraged. When you have talent in a South Wales mining family you don't hide it away, you bring it out for all to see, especially if it is a singing talent. Tom was put into the limelight at family gatherings. They would stand him on his first stage, a chair, and let his talent pour out.

Tom said; 'Among those relatives who encouraged me most was my father's eldest brother George. He had a magnificent voice which was well known not just in Pontypridd but in the surrounding valleys. On Saturday night there was usually a sing song. My parents would bring relatives back to our house in Laura Street for a last drink after an evening at the working men's club.' George, himself a good singer, recognized raw talent, and forced the young Tom out of bed and demanded that he sing for the small audience. Tom, half asleep, would hang his head down but Uncle George gave him his first lesson in showbiz technique, 'No, sing to people's faces, let them see what you are singing about,' he said.

That simple piece of advice not only helped Tom defeat his shyness but kept with him all through his professional singing life.

Years later Tom told a reporter, 'I always wanted to be a singer since I was a child in Wales. In Wales everybody sings because there's a lot of opportunity to sing. People used to say I had a good voice so I was always encouraged to sing.'

It was not only Uncle George who gave the encouragement. His brother Edwin was so confident of Tom's singing talents he took him along to a pub in the nearby town of Llantrisant and stopped the drinkers dead in their tracks. A proud uncle announced Tom's arrival to the assembled drinkers and stood Tom on a chair. Edwin would recall the story in later years. 'He just had to sing to all the patrons. He'd get up and sing a song anywhere.'

When Tom was growing up during the 1940s a World War was going on and factories throughout the valleys and on the nearby Treforest Industrial Estate were doing their bit to turn out components for the war effort. The factories soon became prime targets for the German Luftwaffe determined to put them out of action.

Tom recalled some of his first memories. 'The earliest were of the war years. Of course I was only five years old when it ended but I remember the noise. There was an arsenal not far from our town. The bombers were out for the target but by the time they got to our valley they knew they'd missed out. But they couldn't get back to Germany on their fuel so they had to lighten their load and dump the bombs on us. Adults had gas masks, they were afraid the Germans would drop mustard gas but the masks were too big for the children, so they had protective cages for us. They'd shove the baby in and pump air into it. I can remember the searchlights and there was always guns going off. I suppose at the time I thought that's the way the world was.'

Bombs or no bombs, Germans or no Germans, life had to go on, and Tom Jones was about to give his first concert and get paid for it into the bargain. Just around the corner from 44 Laura Street a short, ginger haired man called Tom Marney ran a little post office and general store in Wood Road, Treforest, which the locals looked upon as a sort of small community centre where they could exchange gossip. Marney had run the shop for donkey's years and one of Tom's uncles had even worked there as a boy. Tom Marney was typical of the many small shopkeepers scattered throughout the valley. He was described as a hard-working, jocular, red faced man who wore a brown overall. Like all valley shopkeepers he was always tapped into the latest gossip and what was happening in Treforest.

Tom Marney had heard about young Tom's singing exploits and as with all local gossip took it with a pinch of salt. He was inquisitive though, and when Tom and his mother visited the shop one day Marney suggested that the lad give him and his customers a song. Freda stood Tom on top of an orange box as a conglomeration of shoppers looked on. They were overwhelmed by the little lad's voice and they congratulated him, saying he was destined to be a star.

Marney, satisfied that all the stories were true, said to the shoppers, 'Come on, give the boy a few coppers.' Freda protested, saying, 'Oh no, I don't want anything for him.' But Marney insisted. 'You can't have talent like that for nothing.' Pennies were pressed into Tom's hand, his first earnings as a singer. Tom said years later, 'By singing I was drawing attention to myself. It was good to be patted on the head for it and receive money for sweets.' Subconsciously, even as a child, Tom had noted that with his talent people would be willing to pay, and that notion would certainly come in handy in the future.

As the stories about Tom's singing spread throughout the village the demands for his voice began to increase. Freda was a member of the Treforest Women's Guild and they would meet in a small hall at the top of Stow Hill. They would say to Freda, 'Bring young Tommy along to sing. 'She would duly oblige and Tom would have them hypnotized with his renditions of 'Mule Train' and other hits of the day. Afterwards the doting ladies would give him cakes and make a big fuss. Soon the word spread and he was invited to sing at children's parties, weddings and village concerts. It would be a good few years before he was famous but to many he was already catching on.

Schooldays loomed over the horizon. At the age of five Tom John Woodward Jnr went to Treforest

Primary School in Wood Road. It was an old fashioned brick building where discipline and emphasis on the 'three Rs' — reading, writing, and arithmetic — prevailed and where each pupil built up his shrewdness and awareness in the tough atmosphere of the school playground.

At school Tom showed he was no great shakes at reading, writing or arithmetic. Indeed this lack of academic talent seemed to haunt him throughout the years he spent at both primary and secondary schools. But even if he was considered dull by academic standards various teachers and fellow pupils realized he was a bit different.

Schoolmate Brian Blackler recalled the early days at Treforest Primary School. 'He can't have been much older than five. The first song I heard Tom singing was "Ghost Riders in the Sky". He sang it in front of the class and he was great. Throughout the years I was at school with him I watched his singing style improve and get even better.'

The teachers were certainly impressed and the young Tom was invited to sing in a variety of school choirs. But singing at the school sometimes had its drawbacks. One irate teacher told Tom off for 'drowning out' other pupils while they were singing the Welsh National Anthem. On another occasion the Woodward voice came across as so 'American Deep South' that the teacher could not believe that this little boy from Treforest could sing in such a fashion. 'I sang the Lord's Prayer in school and the teacher asked me why I sang like a Negro spiritual. I told her I didn't know but I felt it should be sung that way. Then the teacher got all the classes together and asked me to sing in the assembly hall. No one could understand why I sang it like a spiritual and I had no answer for it either,' Tom said.

Tom described his life at home in 44 Laura Street, one of many of those terraced houses that sprawl right throughout the valley, as a 'happy and stable one.' He was surrounded by a family who gave him nothing but encouragement to sing, and during the hard times years later, when he was trying to break into show business, he said this background gave him the strength to carry on. It was a typical mining home where the father would go down the pit and graft all day and the mother would stay at home washing, ironing, cooking and generally being what is accepted as a valley housewife.

In Treforest, even to this day, there is little time for feminism. This sub-culture firmly believes that men and women have clearly defined roles in the family household. Tom said, 'When I was a kid and came home from school I'd never have worried if dad wasn't there. But if the house had been empty and my mother hadn't been there I would have felt it was the end of the world or something. A woman is the most important thing in anyone's home.'

It was an old fashioned valley home life based firmly on hard work and love and respect for each other. When Tom's father came back after a hard day down the pit he would walk proudly up the back path. Between the squeak of the gate and his father coming through the door his food had to be on the table ready for him.

Tom recalled, 'She respected him for it and he in turn respected her because she had everything under control. My mother actually enjoyed doing it, she wasn't forced to do it. She did all her own decorating and took pride in her home and looking after my father. I don't think she would have wanted to do anything else.'

Like most houses in the area, 44 Laura Street had no bath. So after each shift Tom's father, covered in coal dust, would have his tea and bathe in the back kitchen in a zinc bath which always hung on the back of the door. The bath had another use when at midnight on 31 December, Freda and her husband would 'bang in' the New Year on it.

Tom's mother, as most women brought up in the valleys, was a prolific cook. She did a lot of baking, rice puddings, tarts and the inevitable Welsh Cakes (made from eggs, flour, currants and bacon fat) which she baked in a metal pan on the hot stones after raking the coals. Sunday was the big eating day. It was a tradition. The family ate at two, after Tom, Sheila and Freda came back from chapel. Tom Snr joined them after a few pints of beer and a chat with his 'butties' at the nearby Non Political Club. They were a proud family, and no matter how bad the finances they always had a joint of meat on the table.

Freda Woodward might have been the typical Welsh housewife and good at her job, but she did once attempt to be liberated. She took a job in a local factory, much to the disapproval of Tom's father, who didn't like the idea of a woman working. He believed she belonged in the house. One day the family decided to have an outing to the pictures, and as they were waiting outside the cinema a young boy came up to them in the queue and shouted, 'Hello Freda'. Tom's father turned blue with rage. He demanded to know who the boy was. She told him it was a boy who worked at the factory. Tom Snr bellowed, 'You're not going to that factory anymore. If they can't call you Mrs Woodward then you don't work there.'

Apart from being a full time housewife, Freda had another unusual part time job. If anyone died in the area she would be asked to lay them out. This involved dressing-up the deceased person so that he or she would 'look their best' before the funeral. It was another custom in this small village and only given to those who were trusted and highly respected by their neighbours. So it was not an unusual sight to see relatives of the deceased person knocking at 44 Laura Street at all times of night to require Freda's services. It was in this sort of environment Tom was brought up and as he became more street wise and grew older he became more mischievous. His lack of academic understanding led him to rebel and by the time was due to go to secondary school, Treforest Central School, he was playing truant regularly and being punished by his father and mother.

Tom said years later, 'My parents were very important to me. I don't look back on my childhood and think of any bad times. My mother gave me slaps many times but to me it was needed. If I got the hell knocked out of me it was because I asked for it. When you've lived the life of Laura Street you don't forget it.'

For all his shortcomings he still enthralled people with his singing. He was a regular member of the secondary school choir and would sing for his friends and family whenever the occasion demanded. Singing and playing in the streets took up most of his time and he made no real effort to improve his lack of educational ability. Soon he had another two diversions, radio and cinema. 'I sometimes wish I had paid more attention at school. I used to listen to Radio Luxembourg under the bedcovers at night rather than do any homework,' he said.

Radio opened up a whole new world of singing styles, and it was cinema that provided him with the further inspiration to become a performer. Like millions of others Tom was inspired by Larry Parks in The Jolson Story and Jolson Sings Again. 'As a kid I'd watch Larry Parks portray Jolson on film and I decided there was something special about using those mechanisms of dropping to the knee, the outreached arm, the constant movement . I could see that he was completely relaxed and getting across to the audience and I thought, "1 want to be like that"'

It was around this time that Tom, aged eleven, met his first love, lifelong sweetheart and future wife Melinda (Linda) Trenchard. She lived not far from Tom at 3 Cliff Terrace, Treforest. Like other children in the area they would play marbles and other street games together. Each had a crush on the other and this puppy love carried on for several months until a dangerous black cloud loomed over the horizon.

Until not so many years ago tuberculosis killed people by the score. Survivors of this horrible and debilitating disease were usually disabled for life. Tom was about to go to secondary school when he was struck. The family were shocked. After all, the boy had been well brought up, well fed, well looked after; what could have been the cause? In those days TB was a mysterious disease and there was no real answer to all these questions. Freda and Tom Snr were heartbroken as Tom lay in bed seriously ill. The doctor suggested sending him to a convalescent home in Scotland, but Freda and Tom Snr protested saying that they wanted to look after him themselves He was 'too precious' to be carted away to a strange place and be cared for by strangers. After some urgent deliberation it was arranged that the sick boy would be moved to a room at the top of the house where he would get plenty of fresh air. For more than a year Tom lay confined to bed trying to win an uphill battle against the deadly disease. He spent most of his time drawing and painting. To help with his already appalling schoolwork the school arranged for a tutor to give him lessons each day, and ironically under his tutor, a Mrs Warren, he found himself enjoying his school lessons for the first time.

Being confined to bed is no fun for any child but Tom's parents tried to make it bearable and let his free his friends into his bedroom to see him. One of the biggest worries for them was, would the TB affect his voice? Their worries proved to be groundless. Ashe got gradually better Tom would sing for them and his visiting friends just to prove that his vocal chords were still intact Not long after his TB experience Tom was taken on holiday with 0his parents and sister to a caravan in Trecco Bay, Porthcawl. Brian Blackler was invited to come along and it did not take him long to realize Tom was once again back on singing form.

The family had a get together with friends outside the caravan and a sing-song developed. Tom pulled out a small guitar and gave an impromptu performance which proved once and for all his singing talent was still intact.

During his long illness he had been encouraged to eat as much as possible and when he eventually hit the streets again a new style Tom Woodward appeared. Before he had been a short, thin boy with light brown hair but following his eighteen months in bed he was tall, chubby and had black hair. It took him no time at all to get back into the swing of things. At Treforest Central Secondary School he is remembered for frequently climbing over the wall where the girls were and attempting to frighten the life out of them. It was during this time Linda met Tom again and at first sight she did not recognize him. But it was inevitable in their small community that they renewed their friendship and began to hang about with each other again.

Linda recalled later, 'We got together at dances at the youth club and though at this time we were too young to say we were going out together we always seemed to end up with each other.' Over the next couple of years she coaxed Tom to improve his dancing skills and that coupled with his singing ability led people to believe he was destined to go places. The first time Linda realised Tom had an outstanding singing talent was when his sister, Sheila, had her engagement party.

Linda said, 'Tom's mother and mine knew each other well so it was quite natural that when his sister got engaged he should invite me to the party. It was at the party that I first really heard him sing. Tom was the star. He got star billing. He sang "Ghost Riders in the Sky" and accompanied himself by tapping his fingers on the table. I wish it had been recorded. His rhythm was there even at that age.' At secondary school, although a regular concert performer, Tom continued to be no great shakes academically so at the age of fifteen, like hundreds of others, he left and took his first job, making gloves at the Polyglove Factory on the Broadway, Treforest. He vowed that he would never go down the pit after seeing all the men in his area who suffered from coal dust disease which was nicknamed 'the black lung'. Besides, after his TB experience it would not have been wise. Tom's parents wanted him to take up a 'proper job' and learn a trade but he was obstinate like his father and had made his mind up — the glove factory would do for him.

It was 1955, the year that rock and roll was born. Bill Haley, Little Richard, Elvis, Jerry Lee Lewis, Carl Perkins, Fats Domino, our own Tommy Steele, and Marty Wilde were all going great guns. Like thousands of other youths throughout the country Tom decided to merge with this musical revolution and became a Teddy boy. Gangs of the new rock and roll freaks sprang up all over the Pontypridd area. The three main ones were the Rhydyfelin Teds, the Treforest Teds, and the Ponty Teds. Tom wore Edwardian suits with a velvet collar. He listened to a lot of rock and roll and like his friends thought it was considered 'big' to have a girl, drink a lot and fight with other guys. To them it was their contribution to the decade and their part of the rock and roll revolution. It was the 50s sign of being a man.

With the new image came the odd skirmish. In one fight Tom had his nose smashed. 'Kids in our town used their heads when he fought in the streets,' he said. Tom became no amateur in a backstreet rumble. In the 60s he said, 'That's why I hate my horrible nose. It's been worked over, bent sideways and patched up more than any part of me. And always by a head. We liked to keep our hands nice and smooth like.' Neighbours would comment that the Woodward boy 'didn't half fancy himself' as he strutted around the area like a young buck trying to earn his feathers. He would walk past the local club and someone would say, 'Look at that animal'. Tom had to fight to prove himself. He would go haywire and get stuck in. It was considered normal for the times.

The fights came thick and fast. During one over a woman Tom admitted almost beating another man into pulp. A few weeks later he got into a scrap with another fellow who was annoyed because Tom had beaten-up one of his mates. The guy in question was quick off the mark and head-butted Tom through a fish and chip shop window. When Tom scrambled out covered with glass, two policemen were standing there. They said if Tom lifted a finger to touch the other guy they'd run him in. Tom reckoned his nose got broken a couple of times during the fights when anything went — including 'sticking the boot in' and head butting. To be a Teddy boy like Tom you had to use every dirty trick in the book if you wanted to win a street fight in Pontypridd, and when he later became famous he had to have two expensive 'nose jobs' to put the results of his fighting days right.

In those days the Teddy boys got the blame for everything from car thefts to burglary, and the police maintained Tom was a bit of a wild man with a knack for getting himself into trouble. He reckoned he had the kind of face that invited trouble without even trying. He said in the 1960s, 'The police were always on the look-out for me, but I got away with most things, like getting into the cinema without paying. Did he ever get into any other trouble? 'Oh yes, but when the officials came to see my mother with the brass nicely polished in the front room and pictures of Grandad with his medals, they went away saying ' 'no ruffian could live here". Tom had fallen in with a gang his parents and neighbours did not think much of. But he saw it as part of the growing up process and developing his own identity. 'In my teens I used to wear a sky blue suit and black suede crepe-soled shoes. We were all very aggressive. Teddy boys were men with big shoulders. Our girls were aggressive too. They wore lots of make-up and were very tough. That's the kind of thing I grew up with and it's left its mark. Teenagers don't have to be aggressive today because older people aren't fighting them. They can round off the edges.'

After becoming the classic Teddy boy overnight he lived and breathed rock and roll. Although by day he had the mundane job of a trainee glove cutter, at night he would come alive through his clothes and music. Locals who remember him describe him as a smart dresser. He loved fashionable waistcoats and cowboy type ties and wore his hair very long, which was frowned upon by the older inhabitants of Treforest in the 1950s. Linda had a job as a drapery assistant in Pontypridd town and Tom would go down to see her in his finest Teddy boy attire, but the management of the place took a dim view at the sight of him. So anytime they met during shop hours Tom had to keep a low profile.

His mother had terrible battles with him to get his hair cut and only won if she resorted to bribery saying she would buy him a new shirt if he did so. During the 1950s Tom could be seen walking about the streets with a Teddy boy coat with trousers that were reckoned to be as narrow as the thinnest pair of drainpipes in Pontypridd. Tight belts also took his fancy and on one embarrassing occasion this extended even to the cord on his pyjama trousers when he lay in bed one night moaning and complaining of a stomach ache. Fearing that it could be food poisoning, or to do with his TB experience, or something even worse, Tom's mother ran over to the phone box and called the doctor.

When the doctor arrived he took one look at Tom's stomach and loosened the pyjama belt. The tired and overworked doctor shook his head in disbelief. He turned to Tom's mother, pointed to the belt and said, 'That's the cause of his aches and pains. He's tied it too tight.'

The 1950s was the decade of burning yourself out, the age of the motto 'live fast, die young' and like many other young victims of those days things began to move at an alarming rate for Tom. He and Linda had become very close and everyone expected them to marry. It seems to be a sort of tradition in the South Wales valleys for people to marry young. Men are no sooner out of their short trousers and girls discarding their dolls when they are married. Being married young is part and parcel of the Treforest subculture. It is expected of them by their peers and elders. A propagation of the family unit.

If Linda went anywhere and Tom was not there his friends would not allow anyone else to chat her up or bother her, saying, 'Linda is Tommy's girl.' Linda was indeed very much Tommy's girl. They were both aged sixteen when they discovered she was pregnant. The pregnancy came as a shock to both the Woodward and Trenchard families but the fuss quickly simmered down when both announced they were going to do the right thing and marry as soon as possible. Tom and Linda tied the knot at Pontypridd Register Office, Courthouse Street, on 2 March 1957.

Tom described himself as a general labourer and his father put himself down as a coal heaver. Linda gave her profession as drapery shop assistant with her father, William Henry Trenchard, being registered as a motor mechanic. The two main witnesses to the marriage were Ken Davies, Tom's brother-in-law, and Josie Powell, Linda's auntie. It doesn't take a handwriting expert to know that Tom was under extreme pressure. His signature on the wedding certificate is small and cramped, perhaps suggesting that he felt the world was closing in on him and his wild days were over. Here he was a mere boy of sixteen taking on the responsibilities of marriage and fatherhood.

The wedding could not be described as an elaborate affair. About ten people attended the ceremony and then headed off for a quiet drink. Tom later said, 'A lot of my friends got married when they were sixteen or seventeen. You started working at fifteen, many of them in the mines. When you're working you think you're a man. You want to go out drinking with the boys. You want to be an adult. Getting married is part of it. It's proving you're capable. I think I may have felt older then than I do now.'

Tom moved in with Linda and her parents at 3, Cliff Terrace and continued working at his hated job in the Polyglove factory where the only highlight of the day was playing football at lunchtime. He had been mildly interested in making leather gloves but complained he was always given dull jobs and held back from improving. Another negative point was his earning power. At that time he earned thirty-eight shillings (£1.90p) a week while some of his friends were getting four pounds or even more. As a husband and prospective father Tom could see no future at the factory and he looked about for another job.

He found it at the British Coated Board Paper Mills on the Treforest Industrial Estate, he landed a job as a labourer there and surprisingly showed enthusiasm in his work. The management thought he had some potential so he was promoted to a machinist on the paper coating machines. This was unusual as most machinists were aged over twenty-one. As a machinist he had to work twelve-hour shifts from 6a.m. to 6p.m. five days a week or the opposite way round.

Fast growing into a man, and set to become a father at sixteen, he knuckled under to earn money for his new family. He stood out from the other workers. It was embodied in his attitude, an attitude that seemed to say, 'I'm not going to be here for ever'. He had a vivid imagination and he believed that his singing talent would overcome all and make him a star. At weekends he began performing at sing-alongs in the Wood Road Non Political Club.

There was no financial advantage in it. No one paid him but he saw it as a release from his dreary existence and more importantly a way of further building up his singing experience.

Tom was working in the paper mill when Mark was born in April 1957. He recalled, 'I didn't have two halfpennies to rub together. I was excited but my first thought was, ' Can I support him? Will I be able to do him justice?' . I was working nightshift at the paper mill and I couldn't even take a shift off when my wife went into hospital. Just as she was leaving in the ambulance I was going to work on my bike.'

Tom, Linda, and Mark settled in at the Trenchard home in Cliff Terrace. It had been a nerve-racking time for all of them and a lot had happened over the space of a year. Tom's nerves were on edge with all the responsibilities he had to face as a young husband and father, and it was during this time he claims to have had his first supernatural experience. 'The biggest fright I've ever had was in Cliff Terrace when we lived with Linda's parents. We were in bed . . . when there was a terrific bang downstairs. I asked Linda if she heard the noise. She just mumbled sleepily, ' 'It came from outside". The next thing I heard was the heavy tread of someone walking up the stairs. It could have been a burglar and I waited for the door to open. I was ready to jump at him from the bed.

There was a rustling noise but the door remained closed. But after the time it would have taken for someone to walk across the room there was another bang in the wardrobe. I was in a cold sweat and asked Linda if she'd heard the noise. All I got was, "'Don't worry". It wasn't a burglar — so what was it?' Supernatural experience or post-marriage nerves? It was clear the pressures of being married with a young wife and baby were getting to him.

About the same time Tom began to frequent The Wheatsheaf Hotel in Rickards Street. The Wheatsheaf had stood for more than a century and was known as an old-fashioned pub with plenty of atmosphere. It was rather an unusual pub and locals called it 'two pubs knocked into one' as it had three bars: the public bar on the ground floor, the lounge on the second floor and the singing room on the top floor.At first Tom would use the public bar with his mates who included Brian Pittman, Michael Quinn, Dai Perry (who later became his bodyguard), Roy Nicholl, Tony John, Alan Barratt and Brian Blackler, and at weekends a good old sing song would develop. The licencees Jack and Joan Lister decided to make it a feature upstairs in the singing room every Saturday night. They hired a piano player, a local character called Blind Johnny, and things took off from there.

The Wheatsheaf was an ideal place for Tom. It was nearby and provided a unique showcase for his talents. In this old run-down public house Tom began to make a name for himself. Singing all the old time favourites including 'My Yiddisher Mama' which would bring the house down.

The landlady, Mrs Lister, recalls, 'If Tommy was singing, and this is the honest truth, they'd all have silence. Anybody else was singing they would all be talking, they used to be terrible. If you weren't good they were the worst audience in the world, they wouldn't give silence, they wouldn't bother. But if you were good they'd sit and listen. Tom was always the favourite. He was great, we all thought he was wonderful.'

At the age of eighteen Tom was beginning to make his mark on the hard audiences that came to The Wheatsheaf. Soon he became the talk of the valley and people from all over came on a Saturday night to hear him sing. They would cram into the room and be silent as they soaked in with their eyes a boy who had something different — a hypnotic talent. Mrs Lister recalls, 'When Tom was singing they wouldn't even get up for a pint. They'd all just sit there.'

Tom built up his confidence at The Wheatsheaf and at one point joined a local beat group called the De Avalons. Beat groups were springing up all over the area and it was a fashionable thing to do, a chance to make a name for yourself. Tom decided to diversify and began playing the drums but to Tom and the people who came to watch him it was a 'dead loss'. It was just not his natural style, the drums got in the way of his singing and the way he moved his body. In short, drums and their vibrations got in the way of Tom and his gyrations.

As word spread and his reputation built up Tom was asked to join a concert party to sing in clubs at the weekends. Concert party groups had always been popular in the valleys' working men's clubs. Up to half a dozen acts would perform during the course of the night and the clubs would always pay good money. Tom jumped at the chance to make some money from his singing.

There were three acts in the concert party and they called themselves the Misfits. He began to do the round of clubs with them at the weekends and was regularly making £2 a night to boost his young family's income. On one occasion he earned £5 and was left almost speechless with shock.

For the next two years Tom served his singing apprenticeship in the tough and highly critical atmosphere of South Wales working men's clubs with the Misfits. He began to learn new tricks, how to hold an audience, be more professional, and get the best out of his abilities. In his own way he was trying to mould himself into a professional so he could further stand out from all the amateurish and mediocre singers that sang in pubs and clubs throughout the area.

Saturday night he was free and decided to go to a ballroom in Hopkinstown, near Pontypridd, to see Tommy Redman and the Senators perform. Tommy Redman was actually Tommy Pitman, a fellow Treforest lad who lived just around the corner from

Tom. The band had been building up a steady following in the area and Pitman was reckoned to have one of the best voices around. On the night in question Tommy Pitman did not turn up and decided to play cards with his pals instead, so the band were forced to play instrumentals for the first half, which made it a bit embarrassing for everyone. Bass guitarist Vernon Hopkins told the band, 'There's a guy I know who can sing and he's having a pint at the bar.' Tom was asked to fill in and duly bounded on to the stage. The first thing rhythm guitarist Keith Davies remembers Tom saying to him was, 'Do you know "Great Balls Of Fire" in C?' With the infamous words, 'You shake my love but you rattle my brain.' Tommy Woodward and the Senators were off to a cracking start. It was a night when Tom decided to make his singing style more raunchy. 'Before, I'd always just stood there and sung. But this night I started to move in a suggestive way. I can't tell you to this day why I did. It just happened, something inspired me. People stopped dancing to watch me and I began to move even more with a lot of sexy gyrations. The chicks were really excited. It worked then and it's worked ever since. Naturally I have stayed with it. It's like a boxer who finds his left hook is working better than anything else. He naturally goes with the left hook. I go with the sex thing.' The female members of the audience went wild at Tom's hips swinging. They had never seen anything like it. In those days it was considered a trifle obscene, as if Tom was attempting to make love to every female in the audience.

After the successful gig with Tom, the band decided to have a meeting the next day at Vernon Hopkins's house in Rhydyfelin near Treforest. A rehearsal was arranged for the morning. Tom was invited along. During the rehearsal in the front room Tom sang a variety of blues and Jerry Lee Lewis numbers. 'He seemed to be Jerry Lee Lewis mad,' Keith said. Afterwards Tom rather unexpectedly sang a haunting hymn called 'Thora'. Keith and Vernon were somewhat taken aback at this new development. After he left, Vernon asked Keith what he thought. Keith replied half-jokingly, 'I am not sure about a rock singer who sings hymns!' But they were hooked on Tom's charisma. The band had a vote and decided to replace Tommy Pitman with Tommy Woodward. When Tom was offered the role as lead singer in the band he thought carefully before making his mind up. 'I had to come to a quick decision. Was I going to try for the big time and earn very little to start off with, or stick around playing the clubs alone? I was not getting any younger. So I stayed.'

Tom had made the decision to earn less money with this band than with the Misfits; it was a gamble and he hoped it would pay off. He felt bad about leaving the Misfits but managed to pluck up the courage and tell them about the latest developments and surprisingly, although they seemed disappointed, they took it very well. With his new role as lead singer came a new name. Tom called himself Tommy Scott and he and the Senators hit the road. Soon they were playing regular weekday gigs. Abercynon Ballroom on Tuesdays; the Green Fly,

Bedwas on Thursdays; the Memorial Hall, Tredegar varied weekdays; and the YMCA Pontypridd on Fridays. Weekends too were fully booked and they began to play clubs all over South Wales. Keith remembers those early days vividly. 'A lot of groups were around at that time but the Senators were the best because Tom gave us the edge. When we played you could not get a seat.' Tom remarked years later, 'At first it was a losing battle. The kids were used to such tame stuff at the time. But I persevered. I had always been an aggressive singer and suddenly I found I had a big following in South Wales.'

One night Tom went bananas when he heard that his great rock and roll hero Jerry Lee Lewis was playing in Sophia Gardens, Cardiff. He and Keith and a few friends went along to the show and Tom was completely overawed by the performance. After the show Jerry Lee Lewis jumped into a car and sped off. Tom hopped into a taxi and shouted the immortal words, 'Follow that car'. When Jerry Lee's car stopped at the traffic lights Tom leaped out of the cab, banged on the window and got his autograph. Years later they were to become firm showbiz friends in America.

In the early 1960s Chubby Checker began to revolutionize the dance scene by getting everyone to do the Twist. The craze took off in dancehalls all over Britain. To capitalize on this Tom gave himself a new nickname, 'Tiger Tom the twisting vocalist'.

The Senators were riding on the crest of a wave and were demanding, and getting, £12 to £15 per night — not an inconsiderable sum in those days. With all the gigs flowing in Tom felt that he could not hold down his job at the paper mill, with its odd shifts, and be a singer as well. One had to go, and it was the paper mill. He landed a job as a brickie's labourer in Cardiff and took to hod carrying. Tom reckoned the fresh air and running up and down a ladder with a hod would be good for his chest. But after humping bricks all day his mind was still firmly on show business. 'I became interested in show business the moment I realized how heavy a hod was,' he said. His adoring fans would follow the band all over the place. Particular favourites were the Green Fly, Bedwas (where the management were so impressed they offered them a regular Wednesday night gig for months), the Cwm Welfare, Beddau, and the Wood Road Non Political Club where Tom's uncle was chairman and most of his family and friends drank.Tom told DJ Alan Freeman in Rave magazine in 1965, 'There was a lot of people who had faith in me, who gave me confidence. My family, of course, and blokes I knew at work. They used to say, "With your voice you ought to be singing more serious stuff". You know what South Wales is like. Everybody's singing all the time, hymns, chapel, choirs, and miners' clubs.' Tom took heed of their advice but felt that he lacked the musical tuition to put over a serious song well. He sought out a local music teacher for advice and perhaps the off-chance that she would give him singing lessons.

'Do you want to do it for money?' she asked. Tom replied, 'I want to do it because I like it.' The music teacher said, 'Good. I'm not sure that I can teach you to sing any way but your own, but what I can teach you to do is to breathe.' According to Tom, that's exactly what she did, and he emerged from his experience a more polished and professional singer. Although Tiger Tom and the Senators were getting the gigs there was still no sign of big success on the horizon. Tom had improved his voice and jazzed up his act, but still they were stuck in the South Wales club circuit. At one point it drove him to desperation, knowing he had the talent but had not been spotted yet. 'I was thinking, ' 'If I don't make it soon I never will". So I started to take things very seriously.' South Wales was a musical backwater. You could be a genius, brilliant, but the big music boys in London would not come down to see you. It was as if Pontypridd was on a different planet. People would come up after a show and promise wonderful things. 'I know someone who can get a recording contract', or 'I'll get you plenty of regular gigs', but these empty promises spilled out of mouths that usually had too much beer. In the morning, when they sobered up, the boastful drunken promises came to nothing.

For a long time Tom and the band put up with a lot of let downs. He was so down in the dumps one day he said to Linda, 'What do you think, love? Would it be better to pack it in and play it safe?' Linda encouraged him to keep on trying, and a few months later the pop scene began to really take off in South Wales as never before. Clubs with long traditions of keeping rock and roll out of their buildings were now letting the bands in, and that meant more work. For a while Tom gave up his job on the building site and took a part time job selling the latest domestic craze — vacuum cleaners. He was supervised by local character Geoffrey Bloomer, who also taught Tom how to drive. But after a while even that got in the way of the ultimate goal so it was dropped and the band decided to turn professional and work the clubs for a living.

During those formative early days Tom and the band had been given the backing of band member Davie Cooper's father who was the licensee of the Thorn Hotel in Abercynon. But it was two fellow valley boys who were to take over the management side of things. They were nicknamed Myron and Byron. Their real names were Raymond Glastonbury and Raymond Godfrey. Like Tom and the band, they were two go-ahead young men full of youthful enthusiasm. They convinced Tom they could further his struggling career. They knew Tom had an enormous potential. But like Tom they had the disadvantage of being based in South Wales and as time went on this proved to be a great drawback.

They had been trying to get the band on to a recording label but the nearest Tom and the boys got to that was recording a demo tape in the toilets of Pontypridd YMCA, where, according to Keith Davies, 'That's where the acoustics were best.' Early in 1963 Myron and Byron arranged a recording session in London with recording manager Joe Meek. They made a number of recordings including what was proposed to be their first single. The A side was to be 'Lonely Joe' a song written by the Avons, and the B side 'I Was A Fool' written by Myron and Byron. A release date was set and Tom and the boys were promised that the disc would reach the record shops, but it never did. A disgusted Tom went back to London and tore up his contract with Mr Meek and walked out.

Tom was coming out of his hotel room when he spotted Jimmy Savile, the top radio disc jockey of the day with a lot of pull in recording circles. (Years later he had a TV programme called Jim'll Fix It where he made viewers' dreams come true. Perhaps this was his first fix-it.) The eccentric-looking Savile, with long blond hair, big cigar and striped trousers listened as Tom told him he was a struggling singer and asked if he could put the word in for him. Savile said, 'Give me what you have. I'll take it to Decca.' Shortly afterwards Tom was visited in Wales by Peter Sullivan, a recording manager for Decca. Sullivan was very impressed when he heard Tom sing, and promised he would try and get him a recording contract.

But the weeks flew by and Tom and the band became increasingly depressed and desperate. Nothing was happening. Tom went into The Wheatsheaf to drown his sorrows. He told landlord Jack Lister that he had worked hard but was getting nowhere. Jack pulled him a pint and said with the typical optimism of a Welsh landlord, 'Give it another try Tommo. You never know your luck.' Joan Lister remembers that day clearly. 'We always thought Tom would make it. We didn't know when or how, but we always knew he had the talent. All he needed was somebody to push him, a good manager.'

As Tom drowned his sorrows in the public bar of The Wheatsheaf, he could not know that a man he had never met, from up the valley, called Gordon Mills, would soon change the whole course of his life forever.

2. I'll Never Get Over You

If Tom Jones was one side of the success coin, then Gordon Mills was to be the important other side. The Woodward fellow had the singing talent but was flogging his guts out and getting nowhere. Mills was another valley boy who had talent but was waiting for the right chance to exploit it to the full. Gordon was born in India in 1935, the son of a British army couple, Bill and Lorna Mills. His father was a carpenter by trade and rose to the rank of sergeant in the army and during his days in India he was known for playing the clarinet in the army band. Bill was from South Wales but Lorna was Anglo-Indian. After the war was over Bill, a short stocky man some years older than his pretty dark-haired wife, decided to move back to South Wales.

Tonypandy, where they settled. is in many ways similar to Treforest and the environment Tom was brought up in. It made a name for itself more than a century ago when strikers rioted against the injustices of the coal landowners. People remember Gordon as not so much a fighter but as a talker. 'Gordon did not need to lift his hands, he fought with his mouth,' one of his friends Albert Blinkhorn recalled. Like Tom, he was not particularly bright at school but showed an interest in musical things. During the 1950s if you were music mad and relatively poor there was one instrument you could buy to make a sound — the harmonica. Gordon couldn't afford anything fancy like a saxophone or piano so the harmonica was the cheapest way of achieving a musical dream.

At Trealaw Secondary School he told his mate Terry Blinkhorn that he had bought a harmonica and wanted to learn how to play it properly. Terry's brother Albert was well known in the area as an all-round musician who could play the harmonica superbly and gave classes in his Tonypandy home to show local kids how to play it. Albert worked hard with Gordon and five other young men. Soon they had a harmonica band together playing in small clubs for a few pounds a night. Albert said of Gordon during the early days, 'He had a strong character and certainly stood out as an individual. There was no way you could take him off his path if he thought something was right. He had a lot of talent musically and played the harmonica very well. 'Even during those formative days there was one thing everybody noticed about Gordon Mills — he had a tremendous amount of confidence which tended to overwhelm people. 'He always had that go-ahead thing. He was a good organizer and with the other kids of his age he was usually the chief in command. Even then I think he had the makings of an impresario and that type of future. He always said that he would come back one day with a couple of Rolls-Royces or Bentleys parked outside,' Albert said.

'He was a very convincing sort of guy. He could tell you a thing was black and even if you knew damn well it was white, Gordon would convince you it was black. He would gamble on any damn thing and he and his friends would have all-night sessions with cards.' From the age of fifteen Mills began to make his mark on the people around him. He was a good-looking boy, tall and dark, who resembled his mother and was never short of a chat-up line for the girls. But the harmonica seemed to dominate his life and he saw it as a way of escaping the dreariness of the South Wales valleys and making his fortune. After playing a few concerts with the harmonica group Albert Blinkhorn had set up, his next step was to join a local concert party group called the Spades.

The family who made up the group — the Bennetts — were well known throughout the Rhondda Valley for their blend of musical talents. Mrs ('Madame') Bennett played the guitar and sang, husband Sid played the accordion, mandolin and mouth organ, son Frank sang, danced and whistled, and daughter Marjorie had a tremendous voice which later made her a cabaret star abroad. They nicknamed themselves the Spades and in those days it was seen as all-round family entertainment. Gordon was eager to join this unusual family group and began to frequent their house at Western Terrace, Edmondstown. By this time he had built up his harmonica-playing experience and had improved greatly since his first days with Albert Blinkhorn.

When he visited the Bennett household they were surprised and greatly impressed that this young man could copy with ease the great harmonica stars of the day like Larry Adler and Ronald Chesney. The Bennetts voted to have Gordon in the band and soon the young man was getting his first taste of showbiz life playing local pubs and clubs at weekends for the princely sum of fifteen shillings (75p) a night. The youngest member of the family, Johnny Bennett, can remember Gordon coming to the family house brimming with confidence and raring to go with new numbers to rehearse.

The experience of playing with the Spades in the twilight world of Rhondda showbiz had been steadily building up when Gordon left school at the age of fifteen and took on a variety of dead-end jobs in the local steelworks, colliery and motor trade. During the 1950s he was called up to do National Service in the army and like thousands of other young men he went reluctantly. But in a lot of ways it was the best thing that could have happened to him.

After two years in the armed forces he returned to Tonypandy and boasted to his friends that he would escape the rut of the valleys and make it in show business with his harmonica. It seemed his time in the army had made him more confident and determined. He had impressed fellow soldiers with his brilliant harmonica playing and it was they who gave him the extra confidence by saying he should not waste his talent.

When Gordon arrived back in Tonypandy, he was quickly disillusioned by the drabness and boredom of the valley's existence. He told friends, 'I'm going to get somewhere in life, you just wait and see.' Some of them scoffed. It was a common syndrome: a young man leaves the Rhondda Valley to join the army, he meets different people, sees different things, and comes back with his head full of daft nonsense. To his friends, Gordon was in the same boat. No doubt the daft ideas would fade away and he would meet a girl, settle down, and live out the rest of his life in Tonypandy. If Gordon believed otherwise it was going to be a long struggle to prove them wrong. He took a job as a bus conductor with Rhondda Transport, and continued to daydream about breaking into the music game and becoming famous. For ages they were only fantasies, but one day he read in a music paper that the makers of harmonicas, Horner, were staging a British Harmonica Championship at the Albert Hall in London. This could be his big break but at the last moment he had self-doubts. Was he really good enough to meet the challenge? He asked his harmonica teacher, Albert Blinkhorn, who was also working as a conductor on Rhondda Transport, for his advice. Albert had no doubts at all — Gordon was in with a very good chance. A very good chance indeed.

Gordon entered the competition and prepared to travel to London, pawning his prize possession, a radio, to help to meet the cost. The local newspaper, the Rhondda Leader, wrote, 'Gordon Mills is going to bring a frown to every Welshman's face by not singing but going to London and playing harmonica.'

He came second in the championship and made a lot of important show business people sit up and listen. He was sounded out by various agents and came back to the Rhondda Valley confident that he had made his first mark on the London music scene. He would tell fellow bus conductors, 'It's just a matter of time now. I'll be off the buses soon and away to London again, but this time to work.' But still he hesitated. He told Albert Blinkhorn he had met 'a couple of contacts' and had a chance of making it with a harmonica group in London; should he give it all up, his job and home in the valleys, in effect risk everything, and go to London permanently? Was it worth him taking a gamble? Albert gave the best piece of advice he had ever received: 'You've got to take a chance. You've got to take a gamble. If you don't do it now you're never going to do anything.'

Gordon took the advice, gave up his job, and headed again to London. He managed to get an audition with the Morton Frazer Harmonica Gang, a group riding high on the popularity of harmonica music, and much to his surprise landed the job. The Gang was to give him a good grounding in the workings of the professional showbiz game. Playing with the Bennett family had been a springboard and an experience in itself, but this was a completely different set-up, dealing with shrewd agents, club owners and ruthless audiences who paid for and demanded the best. Gordon earned £14 a week and most of his time was spent on the road with the band.

The Gang were not only great favourites with the British public, they also went down well with the thousands of US soldiers stationed in this country, and American Army camps were where they tended to play their most profitable and successful gigs.

They regularly appeared on TV and the Bennett family were astounded when they spotted their former member on screen playing with them.

In the late 1950s Gordon made a visit home to his parents in Trealaw, Tonypandy. He called in to see the Bennett family, and Johnny Bennett remarked, 'I saw you with the Morton Frazer group on TV and you were great. Are you still with them?'
Gordon exuded self-confidence. 'Oh no. I've left them. I've formed a group called the Viscounts.' This was even more of a surprise because the Viscounts had just had a hit called 'Mama's Little Baby Loves Shortening Bread.' The Bennetts asked who had done the singing. 'It was me,' Gordon said. They were baffled — as far as they knew Gordon had never sung a note in his life.

It was while Gordon was singing and playing harmonica with the Viscounts that he bumped into a struggling singer called Gerry Dorsey. Arnold George Dorsey was born in India on 2 May 1936. His father Mervyn was an engineering consultant who left the Midlands with his wife Olive to work in India on a Government project. Dorsey was the second youngest of ten children, and was brought up in India until he was eleven.

When the young Dorsey moved to England with his family in 1947 he found the war-torn atmosphere quite different from that of Madras. It was the days of ration books, and austerity still reigned through Britain as though the war had not really ended. Dorsey was brought up at a semi-detached house in

Stroughton Street, Leicester and went to the Melbourne Road Secondary Modern School. If one looks closely at his early life, one can see great similarities between Tom and Gordon. At school Gerry was considered a flop and years later admitted he was almost always at the bottom of the class. Because of his introverted nature he claimed teachers and bullies made life hell for him. One school report on Dorsey, aged 12, said that he was a 'very shy boy suffering from innumerable complexes'. Although, like Tom and Gordon, not academically bright, he did have a penchant for music. During his early teens his father bought him a saxophone and it was his great dream to emulate his namesake, Jimmy Dorsey, the great saxophone player of the day. Gerry Dorsey took music lessons and his saxophone playing gradually got better. But family pressure steered his ambition away from any daydreams of stardom to more sensible things like finding a 'good job' when he left school. After leaving school he went to college for a while and then joined a local engineering firm as an apprentice. But the money was extremely poor and Dorsey felt within his heart he did not want to follow in his father's footsteps as an engineer.

So he gave up his apprenticeship and took on a semi-skilled job in a Leicester boot and shoe factory earning £4 a week. Tom had found a release through his singing, Gordon through his harmonica, and Dorsey was to find it first of all through his sax. In his spare time he practised hard and when he went down well at a couple of small parties it gave him more of an appetite to try harder. He and his brother

Eddie began getting small gigs at working men's clubs. When he appeared on stage he found that people would shout 'Give us a song' and he would be encouraged to put down his saxophone and sing to them. His voice certainly worked and the applause gave him his first real taste of showbiz excitement. From then on he realized the saxophone would have to take second place to his singing. For the sake of the showbiz game he called himself Gerry Dorsey. He worked hard at it and the bookings began to come in from social clubs all over the Midlands.

When he was called up to do two years' National Service it gave him the chance to experience responsibility and discipline which would ultimately help to develop his basically insecure character. He became a lance corporal in the transport section and served for a time in Germany. But, more importantly, the Army also helped him develop his singing talent. He was asked to sing and play in the NAAFI and at camp concerts and he was encouraged to do something with this talent when he left the army. It was the same story as Gordon. Once he left the army, with great expectations, he found himself in a rut again. He took up a job at another boot and shoe factory but his heart was not in it. He was continually late and the management became annoyed about his attitude to work.He took some time off to attend a talent contest in the Isle of Man and beat a variety of strange and mediocre acts to come away with the first prize of £75. When he came back he received a letter saying he had been sacked. It was as if everything was pushing him towards the bright lights of London and he decided to take advantage of these omens. With a small suitcase Gerry bade farewell to his family and headed for London. For the next few days he tramped around London trying to sell himself to a multitude of showbiz agents. But to many he was just another face, just another singer, amongst a sea of hopefuls, and he was turned away. But eventually he was lucky. One talent spotter did like the look of him and after an audition Dorsey was signed up by Foster's Agency in the West End. Like hundreds of other hopefuls at the time, Dorsey began to be 'groomed for stardom' and was kitted out with the latest pop gear. It was a big money situation. If one hopeful could make it through and become a star the investment would be worth it.

A recording contract with Decca was arranged and his first single 'Mr Music Man' was released. But it flopped and disappeared without trace. The next release was a cover version of the Johnny Ray song 'I'll Never Fall in Love Again' which did marginally better. Although it made no mark in the charts, some important music people did take notice and Dorsey was booked to do several spots on the TV Show Oh Boy. But even that did not make Dorsey a star overnight. To make a living he had, like thousands of other struggling singers, to do the 'bread and butter' gigs all over the country in a plethora of working men's clubs.

It was at such a club in Coventry that he met Gordon Mills. Mills was playing harmonica and singing with the Viscounts. That night Dorsey had planned to sing a song called 'Personality' in his act but he was informed the Viscounts were to do the same song. He backed down and let Gordon and the band perform it.

When Gordon and Dorsey got talking they discovered not only they had the same interests and ambitions in life but they had virtually been brought up in the same sort of background. They were two young men trying to make it big in London and soon this common aim led to them sharing a dilapidated flat together. They paid £4 a week to a Polish landlord for a place that was so damp the wallpaper was peeling, there was hardly any furniture, and the cooking facilities centred around one gas ring. A railway track thundered nearby.

The situation became intolerable and they did a moonlight flit with Dorsey carrying all the bags down three flights of stairs and disappearing into the night. Mills found them alternative accommodation in a house that was full of aspiring artistes trying to make the big time. The house in Cleveland Square was only marginally better than the seedy flat.

Times continued to be hard. At one point Dorsey was reduced to pawning his saxophone. He and Mills would sometimes eat at a cheap café behind Paddington Station when the going was good.
But the poverty of being a struggling singer took its toll on Dorsey. He collapsed one night and when rushed to hospital was found to have TB. Mills said later he thought that was the end of his pal as far as

showbiz was concerned. Everyone thought Dorsey would never sing again.

Dorsey spent more than seven months confined to bed in hospital and had to undergo a further long period of recuperation. Meanwhile Gordon forged ahead with his own life. For a brief moment the Viscounts did well and had their fair share of TV spots which were abundant in the 1960s. But Gordon was fed up with all the travelling, the days on the road, performing in front of couldn't-care audiences and dealing with dodgy club owners. He saw the future in song writing, and left the group. The move showed all his growing self-belief, especially as he could not actually read music. Despite that handicap, however, the hits began to come: songs such as 'Hungry for Love' and 'I'll Never Get Over You' for Johnny Kidd and the Pirates; Cliff Richard's 'I'm The Lonely One' and the Applejacks' 'Three Little Words'.

Over this time Gordon had met and married beautiful fashion model Jo Waring. He asked Gerry Dorsey to be the best man. A few months later, on 18 April 1963, Dorsey decided he wanted to marry his girlfriend and fiancée of long standing Pat Healy. Pat was a secretary from Leicester, who had met Gerry Dorsey at a Midlands dancehall. He asked Gordon to be the best man and Jo also had her part to play — she designed Pat's wedding dress.
For a while Gerry and Pat lived in a room at Gordon's flat but seeking independence they moved out to a shabby flat in Hammersmith High Street. Gordon's career had been a struggle but he was certainly doing far better than his contemporary,

Dorsey. They lost track of each other for a while as Gordon, between song writing, landed himself a job as an assistant recording manager with a record company. But even at this stage Gordon could never have been considered well off: there were hundreds of budding songwriters in London all vying for a place in the charts and the going was tough.

Gordon decided he would chance his hand at management once the 'right act' came along. He decided the act would have to be something different and dynamic, something that would enthral audiences with its power and in the end make a lot of money. But to Gordon's dismay there seemed to be nothing new emerging in London.
If something did turn up, he discovered the act was already with another management and had already signed a contract. There had to be someone out there who could set the charts alight but where were they? To Gordon it was a frustrating game. He spent many nights searching London clubs and pubs for such an act but it seemed to be in vain. Meanwhile more than a hundred miles away in Pontypridd, and just six miles down the road from Gordon's home village of Tonypandy, the young Tommy Scott got drunk and dreamt of the day he would become a star. Gordon became increasingly angry and disillusioned with the British pop scene. It was 1964, the height of the Beatles and Rolling Stones. There were other bands and solo artistes, but it all seemed so predictable. During this time, Tom had been forging ahead in South Wales under the guidance of managers Myron and Byron. After seeing Tom for the first time at a local club, Johnny Bennett realized that this lad

from Treforest had a lot of potential. After the show Johnny got talking to him and mentioned that he was a friend of Gordon Mills. Tom was impressed; after all, Gordon was a songwriter in London and perhaps he could do some good. 'Why don't you get him to come and listen to me and the boys?' Tom said. When Gordon Mills and his wife Jo came to Trealaw for a weekend Johnny Bennett saw it as a golden opportunity for both men to meet. He told Gordon about Tom, saying, 'Why don't you come and listen to this mate of mine?' A sceptical Gordon said, 'What does he do? A singer? They're ten a penny. Who's he like?' Johnny reassured him that Tom was a bit different and unlike anyone playing in the valleys. 'He's original. A cross between Little Richard, Frankie Vaughan and a few others. He can sing a ballad like no one I know and can belt out rock and roll numbers.' Gordon reluctantly said he would go and see Tom.

On the morning of 10 May 1964 Johnny Bennett arranged to pick up Tom and band members Vernon Hopkins and Dave Cooper from Pontypridd and take them to the Lewis Merthyr Club in Porth. When Gordon walked into the club with his beautiful wife Jo they joined Johnny and his wife, schoolmate Gordon 'Gog' Jones and his wife, at the table. Gordon asked, 'Where's this Tommy Scott.?' Johnny pointed to Tom sitting at the other end of the table wearing a leather jacket. 'What, that scruffy bastard?' Gordon exclaimed. 'Half a moment,' Johnny said. 'You're back in the valleys now. You don't think he goes on stage like that, do you? He dresses when he goes on stage. 'Gordon was introduced to Tom for the first time. Tom told Gordon he was playing the Top Hat Club in Cwmtellery that night and why didn't he come along? Gordon agreed. The Top Hat Club was not the most salubrious place but it was popular with the locals. Tom built up one of his strongest followings there. Tom was due on stage at seven.

They got to the Top Hat Club early, but even then his popularity was evident: the club's concert hall was packed out and they could not get in. The man at the door pointed out it was for members only and anyway there were no more seats left. Gordon, Johnny and Gordon Jones headed for the other bar in the club with their wives. Johnny was embarrassed as he had dragged them all that way to see Tom perform, and tried to get Tom's help. The singer came from backstage to plead with committee members: 'That's Gordon Mills the songwriter from London, he's come to listen to me.' One of the committee men relented saying, 'If that's the case tell them to come in. But tell them to keep out of the way or we'll have the members complaining. ' Tom started the show off with the song 'Spanish Harlem', Gordon and his party standing by the door and being jostled by people coming and going. It was more uncomfortable for Jo Mills than the rest of them — she was distinctly pregnant. Tom did half an hour of his rip-roaring act, but Gordon showed no emotion. Then came comedian and singer Bryn Phillips who specialized in such songs as Perry Como's 'I Know'. After Tom had completed the second half Johnny asked Gordon what he thought. Gordon shook his head and said, 'No.' He added with a smile, 'The bloody comedian's not a bad singer, though.'

A disillusioned Johnny asked Jo what she thought of Tom. 'Do you want to know the truth?' she said. 'I don't know what this boy is doing in a club like this. He's too bloody good.'Johnny said, 'Gordon didn't seem to think so.'Jo laughed and replied, 'If Gordon didn't think so he would have gone after the first half.' Johnny had the feeling that Gordon was playing games with him. He looked straight into Gordon's eyes and said, 'Come on, let's have a bit of common sense. Are you trying to tell me that comedian can sing better than Tom?'

Gordon laughed. He had been playing a game. He said to Johnny, 'Can you get hold of Tom for me?' Tom's managers, Myron and Bryon, who were two heftily-built lads, could sense that something was in the air and they eyed Gordon suspiciously. According to Johnny, Myron came over to him and said as he stood by the door, 'Hey that's Gordon Mills isn't it?' Johnny nodded, saying yes. Myron glared at him saying, 'Well, tell him to piss off.' 'Hey, wait a minute,' Johnny retored, 'there's no need for upsets. If anybody can do anything for Tom it's this boy here. He's well in with Decca and he's writing songs. Why don't you get together and sort something out?'

Although Gordon had remained cool and aloof that night, he later confessed that he had never seen anything like Tom. To Gordon, Tom was an uncut diamond who needed polishing and Gordon saw himself as the man who could do the job and create a star.

'The lad was sensational,' he said later. 'He had the audience in a frenzy. I saw in Tommy Scott a potential success. All he needed was to get out of that pitiful mining country to where his talents would be more highly appreciated. The first few bars were all I needed to hear. They convinced me that here was a voice which could make him the greatest singer in the world.'

Gordon met Tom after the show and put it to him straight: if he wanted to become a star he was wasting his talent, energy and time in the valleys — he would have to go to London.

Tom said later, 'It's like what you see in the movies. He looked at me when I got off stage and said, ' 'My God! Gotta take you to London. Gonna get you this, that and the other". Gordon said something and proved it. A lot of people say, ' "You should be doing this. You are this, that and another", but nobody did anything. He saw, and he did.

'A lot of people had given me encouragement but Gordon was the one — the real turning point.'

Gordon and Tom certainly seemed keen to join forces, but there was one problem — the management of Myron and Byron.

If they objected it could put a damper on things. Gordon talked things over with them. He told them London was Tom's best move and he had contacts in the music business there. Myron and Byron were sceptical, they had helped build up Tom's popularity in South Wales, and they were not prepared to lose him without a fight, but they could not argue with Gordon's claim that he had contacts in London where the music business was really happening.

The next meeting they had was about seven weeks later at the Hibs Club in Ferndale, Rhondda. Gordon had been back in London and had told everyone about his new find. Tom had been on his mind consistently. He was convinced that Tom could make it big if only he'd agree to move to London. At the Hibs Club, Gordon outlined his plans to Tom and his two managers. A contract was drawn up giving Gordon managerial control over Tom, with Myron and Byron getting a cut of future royalties.

Gordon, taking over the management from Myron and Byron had been the major hurdle and he saw it as the first stones being laid on the road to success. The next hurdle was Tom himself. Although Tom believed he had had a lucky break meeting Gordon, he was not totally convinced that he should go and stay in London. It meant he would have to leave his family in Cliff Terrace, and they might struggle financially if he gave up his regular South Wales work. Gordon reassured him, saying that he would be looked after and he did not have to worry about money until he became successful. This was primarily a bluff. Gordon was not that well-off and lived in a small flat in London. Albert Blinkhorn recalled, 'I don't think Gordon had a lot of influence at the time, but he had a lot of go-ahead and very little cash. He told me he had only £250 in the bank and an old broken down Cortina.' Gordon may have spun a fancy line, but eventually, although worried about his family, Tom agreed to go to London with him. The night before they left they had a farewell drink at a pub in Pontypridd. Gordon's two friends Gordon 'Gog' Jones and Albert Blinkhorn were also there. Albert remembers Tom having some trepidation about giving up everything and heading for London. Over a few pints he gave him a bit of a lecture about what to do and what to avoid in the big metropolis.

When Tom arrived in London he was armed with a new name. Out went Tommy Scott — and in came Tom Jones. Gordon felt that the name change was necessary as a Tommy Scott was already recording in London. Besides, the name Tom Jones was more fashionable and trendy. It had been the title of a successful movie starring Albert Finney that year, and that could not be bad for business. Along with the new name, Gordon instructed Tom to wear more seductive clothes to increase his sex appeal. Tom also had to appeal to London record producers who were on the lookout for new-style acts. During this first stage Gordon worked hard to promote his man and got Tom his first gig under his management: not in London but in Swansea — only forty miles up the road from Pontypridd. The next move was to bring Tom's group up to London, and they asked Mike Roberts, lead guitar, Chris Slade, drummer, Vernon Hopkins, bass guitar, and Dave Cooper, rhythm guitar, to join them. All of them voted to go except lead guitarist Mike Roberts. He had just landed a good job with a local TV station and decided it was not worth the gamble to give everything up and head for London. Gordon and Tom decided to audition in Wales for a replacement and publicity was placed through the local newspapers.

The auditions were held at the Thorn Hotel, Abercynon, to find a new lead guitarist. More than twenty people turned up and out of these they selected Micky Gee. So it came to be that the band headed for London with high hopes but very little money. Gordon managed to secure loans from the bank and friends to subsidize this make-or-break venture and arranged for the band to move into a flat at Notting Hill. The place was so filthy, damp and dowdy the band soon nicknamed it Calcutta after the Black Hole of Calcutta. Local ladies of the night would often pop into see Tom and his band for a chat and a cup of tea. To tie in with the new bold London image Gordon named the band the Playboys and the neat title of 'Tom Jones and the Playboys' began to be spread around town. But the gigs were slow in coming.

One that Gordon did get them was a regular spot in an Oxford Street club called Beat City (they found supporting the big-name groups like the Rolling Stones, mind-blowing; you did not get chances like that in the Rhondda) but still there was barely enough money coming in to keep them going. Promoting Tom and the band was an uphill task, Gordon found, despite the demo discs they were making. 'People gave me all kinds of stories,' he recalled. 'They said Tom shouted and screamed. They said he was too old fashioned. They said he moved too much like Elvis Presley.'

Excuses, excuses! But Gordon, Tom and the boys gritted their teeth and kept on trying.

3. It's Not Unusual

It did not take long for Tom and the band to become disillusioned with their lot in London. Before, they had been big fish in the little pond of South Wales; now they were small fish in a giant musical pond. There was so much competition, so much talent, they felt they were banging their heads against brick walls. Tom became desperate. Was this really going to be his last chance to make the big time Things didn't work out well,' he said. 'The Beatles had just arrived and the Rolling Stones, so the group scene was very big. My wife had to go to work in Wales to support her and my son, because I wasn't making any money in London. And that upset me because I was brought up to believe that the man goes to work and provides It was on my mind to go back to Wales.' Back in Treforest the gossips were having a field day. 'That Tommy Woodward living it up in London while poor Linda has to go out to work to keep the family,' they would say The group continued making demo discs and playing small gigs around London. Meanwhile the cost of keeping five grown men in a flat in Notting Hill was creating a financial burden for Mills. His overdraft was growing at an alarming rate and he had to resort to paying Tom and the boys one pound a day to feed themselves and pay for everything else Tom and the lads were constantly hungry and during one bad phase, when they had no gigs, they only had half a crown (12^1hp) between them. Tom and another member of the band elected to go out to a café and buy sandwiches with the half a crown. On the way, they dropped the money and thought it had fallen under a grid. Luckily, after much searching, they found it. They went to the café but were so hungry they ate the sandwiches on the way back to the flat. The other members of the band were not too happy about Tom's story that he had lost the money.

Starvation is a quick way of getting your head out of the clouds and jolting you back to reality, and the band began to complain to Gordon about their situation. After all, most of them had steady jobs back in Wales earning at least £15 per week and playing gigs meant another tenner on top of that. But now they had been reduced to living on half a crown between them.

Tom felt increasingly depressed. He said later, 'It was the worst nightmare of my life. I felt I couldn't go back and face everyone as a failure — the guy who had left to make it in the bright lights having to return busted. I just knew I couldn't take it, even if the others could and I decided to hang on for one last-ditch attempt.'

Life on the road also had its ups and downs. On one occasion the band were heading for a one night stand in Birmingham in an old van. Tom had been given a plastic tiger's head for luck from one of his fans at a previous gig. He decided to hang the tiger's head in the van as they headed along the M1.

A few minutes later the van had a puncture and they all got out to repair it. A few miles along the motorway they had another puncture. The van eventually got to Birmingham in one piece.

On the way back after the gig they had another puncture but this one nearly killed all of them. They were doing seventy miles an hour then they heard the screeching of burnt rubber, and the van careered from side to side on the Ml. Fortunately they managed to stop the vehicle just in time and no one was injured. Everyone inside the van looked at the tiger's head. Tom grabbed it and threw it out of the window saying 'Sorry, fan.' Superstition plays a big part in the showbiz world — even at that level.

However, Gordon's hard work was paying off. Record executives at Decca had been somewhat sceptical at first of this new act, Tom Jones, but decided that there might be something to him after all. Gordon announced to an overjoyed band that they were to record their first single, 'Chills and Fever'. This was it! Tom and the band worked hard in the studio and were confident that the single would at least make a ripple in the national music charts. 'Chills And Fever' was released in August 1964, but it did nothing. No ripple. Nothing. The best it could do was register number five in the Pontypridd pop chart which was compiled by a little music shop. But nationally it bombed into obscurity. A new depression hit them all and they went back to recording demo tapes of songs for the big stars. It really got to Tom so much that he contemplated throwing himself under a train at Notting Hill tube station. 'I was standing in the tube station and I thought how easy it would be just to finish everything there and then. I think everyone goes through spells like this. You appreciate the good things later when you look back on the times you were desperate.' Apart from managing Tom and the band, Gordon Mills had been busy with Les Reed writing a song for pop singer Sandie Shaw. The song was called 'It's Not Unusual'. If anything, the lyrics and music sounded predictable enough — 'It's not unusual to be loved by anyone, It's not unusual to be sad with anyone . . .'

Tom and the band were asked to record the demo of the song for Sandie Shaw — the top female singer of the day, whose trademark was to appear barefoot on stage. Tom instantly liked the sound of it. When he heard the playback his intuition told him he must have it. He told Gordon and Les Reed that it could be his first hit. A long argument developed and Mills and Reed stuck to their guns, saying it had been written specifically for Sandie Shaw.

Then Sandie Shaw's management rejected the song, and it fell into Tom's lap. This was definitely the last chance Tom and the boys had. Decca had been none too impressed with the flop of 'Chills and Fever'. Tom said of 'It's Not Unusual', 'It's funny. With this particular song something was telling me all the time, "Don't let it go, this is it"' Gordon decided to play a ruthless move. He believed Tom had a major talent but blamed the band for the flop of the last single. He decided to drop them for 'It's Not Unusual', and the professional recording group the Ivy League were recruited to do the backing on the record.

But there were to be problems. When Tom did the first recording of 'It's Not Unusual' at the Decca studios it just did not sound right. Tom recalled, 'We recorded it with just a few different instruments. It didn't go. We were looking for a sound and we weren't getting it. I felt like death. 'The frustration was evident in the studio until Peter Sullivan, (the producer who had been impressed by Jones when he saw him in Wales), said, 'I know what it needs. I want brass.' Tom thought, 'This is a bit dodgy. Maybe the teenagers won't go for brass.' He decided to try it anyway and was instantly pleased with the result. Much to Tom's relief the brass section gave it an extra dimension and the song sounded good.

Gordon returned home to Trealaw and let his parents and the Bennetts hear the demo disc of 'It's Not Unusual' and the flip side 'To Wait for Love' written by Burt Bacharach. It was like a Rhondda Juke Box Jury. Gordon's mother and Johnny Bennett liked 'To Wait For Love', as Tom always sounded good when singing a ballad, but they all agreed that 'It's Not Unusual' had a more commercial sound to it. 'It's Not Unusual' was released in January 1965 along with 'To Wait for Love'. It proved to be a very lucky time for Tom. As soon as the song was released it began to get steady airplay.

Top British DJ Alan Freeman began playing it on his Sunday night Radio Luxembourg programme. He said of the record, 'I can't remember when I played a new disc on the air with a greater sense of recognizing a pop landmark.' Along with the airplays came an invitation to appear on the TV pop programme Top Gear. It was while Tom was rehearsing for the show that the producer, Bertie

Andrews, told him that 'It's Not Unusual' had come in at number twenty-one in the pop charts. Tom froze with shock. He couldn't do anything for a minute or two. It was the most exciting moment of his life.

On the strength of the record's growing popularity Gordon managed to get Tom and the band numerous bookings up and down the country. Not long after the single splashed into the charts they were playing a club in Bradford and were staying at a local pub cum guest house. Tom and the boys were sitting in the bar having a few beers and playing darts when a man with new records for the juke box came in. Amongst the records was 'It's Not Unusual'. Soon the place was filled with lorry drivers and locals and they began to play the disc. People began to ask who this new singer, called Tom Jones, was. The barmaid pointed over to Tom and said, 'That's him there.' Tom felt himself go deep red with embarrassment but he was glad that locals seemed to like the single. From Bradford to Treforest the single was catching on. Tom's mother and sister would be greeted by friends and neighbours in the street shouting, 'It looks like your Tom's made it at last!' The whole community of Treforest, and indeed, the whole of South Wales was buzzing with excitement that one of their sons could perhaps make it to number one in the charts.

There was no stopping the disc. It jumped up to number eighteen and then leaped up to number two within a couple of weeks. One music critic wrote, 'This is not one record, it is one and a half. I have never heard someone give that much, be it from himself or his voice.' This rather strange pop song with its brass section and relatively unknown singer seemed to capture the heart of the nation. In four weeks it sold more than 800,000 copies. Tom was in demand everywhere. He and his band hit the road. (The band had meanwhile changed their name to the Squires as there was another group called the Playboys recording in London). To add extra effect Gordon added two trumpets and a saxophone to obtain the big sound of 'It's Not Unusual' in the stage act. At twenty-four Tom was reckoned to be 'an overnight success' and hailed as being one of the quickest rises to pop fame ever. He was booked for pop programmes such as Ready Steady Go and Juke Box Jury. Tom said at the time it was as though he had spent years in the dark and then suddenly someone had opened a door and thrown a huge ray of light on to him. Being cast into the limelight and experiencing fame was an unbelievable step for him. He also had to get used to money pouring in for the first time.

During his son's rise to fame Tom's father went down the pit as usual, just as he had done all his working life. After one shift he came up to daylight and got the surprise of his life. He said, 'It was a Sunday when I got to the surface. After my shift some of my mates gave me the big news.' 'Your Tom's got to number one", they said. And there in the Sunday Mirror was the proof.'

To make things even better for the Welsh community Tom's hit was number one on Saint David's Day, 1 March 1965, a time for local and national celebrating. It was also a good omen for Linda. The hit coincided with their eighth wedding anniversary.

Tom's father went home after the shift and invited all his neighbours and friends into 44 Laura Street. They celebrated with whisky, beer and champagne. The next day there were said to be quite a few sore heads in the Treforest area. Tom himself could not believe his luck. After all these years of struggling in pubs and clubs he had finally done it. He said at the time, 'I suppose it has been a bit shattering. It is astonishing how one song can change your life. Suddenly you find yourself in demand from every part of the country. It's flattering and I cannot pretend that I don't like it.

'The success of the song did surprise me a bit. I knew it was a good one and had tremendous faith in it but one reason I thought it might not get to the top is that I suspected the teenagers might not go for it. In point of fact they liked it a lot.' Even Gordon Mills and his wife Jo could not really believe it. The thing seemed to snowball out of proportion. A fan club was set up and 500 applications flooded in. Jo Mills took over the role of spokeswoman and organizer of the club. She said, 'It was a big risk using a backing type band instead of a group but it turned out to be the right thing.'

Although the celebrations were in full swing Linda felt deflated as she sat with her son Mark in the terrace house at 3 Cliff Terrace. Officially she and Mark did not exist. Gordon Mills realized that to be a big star you had to appear unobtainable, beyond reach. It was all part of the sex symbol thing. If you appeared to be single, women would come to see you. But if it got out that you were married, well, it could put thousands of women off. So Tom was given his order by General Mills: 'Keep your marriage quiet for now.'

The plan worked. Tom with his gyrating pelvis, tight trousers, and suggestive movements turned women on in their thousands. The pop industry had not seen anything like it since the heyday of Elvis Presley. Here in Britain at last was the successor to Presley. A man who looked like a man and seemed to want to go to bed with the whole female audience. So in any interviews or references to Tom regarding romance, Mills instructed that the word 'marriage' was out and 'single' be used at all times.

At the time if anyone had to make a British comparison with Tom the name P. J. Proby always seemed to crop up. Proby was renowned for having a very raunchy act. He was reckoned to be way over the top when it came to titillating his female fans, so there were similarities with Tom. But the punchline to Proby's performance was to split his pants, which would disgust some but would have others screaming.

He had been warned about this practice by the management of numerous concert halls and clubs all over the country but he still insisted on splitting his pants as a defiant gesture. He saw it as an idiosyncratic way of giving the V sign to authority and at the same time exciting his audience.

Perhaps he felt his status threatened, but Proby lashed out at Tom in the media in words to the effect that Tom was not in the same league and was merely a copycat who could never become a sex symbol as big as him. Tom and Gordon Mills were annoyed. After all, there was room enough for both of them. Proby had made it, so why not give Tom his chance instead of shooting him down? Tom lashed back at Proby in the newspapers saying he did not copy anybody — least of all Proby.

If there was to be the equivalent of the shootout at OK Corral between the two sex symbols, that chance happened when both were invited to take part in an all-celebrity concert in aid of spastics on Sunday 21 March 1965 at the Empire Pool in Wembley, London. Tom said before the concert, 'It bugs me the way people constantly compare Proby and me because we really are different performers. Now at last I have the chance to prove my point.'

Perhaps this musical showdown was really a publicity gimmick for both stars; in any case Tom emerged as the clear winner. The reviews the next day came out in favour of Tom who they exclaimed to be an exciting new star. Gordon and Tom were pleased, they believed they had won the musical shootout. After the show Proby and Jones shook hands and talked. Much to their surprise they found each other agreeable company. The 'battle' had been largely media hype, but it was all part of the pop game and there was no doubt it had helped Tom sell more records.

The two men's paths were to cross again. Proby was on a major British tour with Cilla Black and had been warned in no uncertain terms that he must refrain from splitting his pants. So what did he do? He went out and split his pants in front of thousands of fans. It was the final straw, the promotors of the tour dropped Proby and looked about for a replacement. They did not have to look far — it had to be Tom Jones. Gordon and Tom did not want to be seen jumping on the Proby bandwagon and taking advantage of the situation, but what else could they do? Here was a golden opportunity to go on tour with a popular established pop star — Cilla Black — and catapult themselves further into the big time.

A lot of Proby's fans were not pleased with the move. The first time Tom joined the tour and went on stage he was taken aback when he glanced at the first few rows. They were full of fans holding up pictures of Proby. A bit shaken with this turn of events, Tom continued with the show and after a while Proby's fans went wild over Tom's singing and hip swinging. By the end they had dropped their pictures of Proby and had been won over to Tom. Such is the ephemeral nature of the pop world.

How do you know when fame hits you? Does someone walk up to you and say, 'Hey, you're famous'? Of course not. Fame works in its own mysterious ways. To Tom, fame meant hundreds of women screaming and shouting at him, but that's as far as it went. Fame to him was when he was on stage performing. But one night during the tour he was having a drink in a pub near the theatre when a group of screaming women burst in. Tom's first reaction was that it had to do with Cilla or one of the other stars in the show. But he was wrong, he had miscalculated the fame game. The screaming women ran over and tore Tom's overcoat to pieces. He managed to escape and ran as fast as he could, hotly pursued by the hysterical females. He only made it back to the stage door by a hair's breadth.

His comment: 'That was my first taste of crowd hysteria and I walked right into it not knowing that it was me they had been shouting at.'

Life on the road had further surprises in store. Once, Tom was travelling down the M1 with Dave Allen the comedian when they stopped off at a motorway café to get a bite to eat and answer the call of nature. Tom, who had been sitting on the bus for hours, rushed to the toilet. On his way there he was spotted by a bunch of girls and they quickly decided to go after him. Tom was mortified, it seemed there is no privacy at all for a pop star. He said, 'Basically there are two things you can do in the toilet and I was literally caught with my pants down. I was sitting there minding my own affairs and these girls jumped over the top of the door.' With his pants still down around his ankles, Tom went haywire, pushing the girls out of the toilet. Quite understandably he was shouting and swearing at them — and they actually took exception to his language and complained about his manners!

'I told them if this was their way of calling on me, I didn't care if they didn't buy my records anymore, just as long as I could go to the toilet. That was the most embarrassing experience I ever had.'

Tom made a triumphant return to Wales and the hordes turned out to greet their hero. Friends, relatives, neighbours, and people from all over South Wales came to see his concert. Linda and Mark were amongst them, and it was during this time the 'big secret' broke.

For months, following the edict of Gordon Mills, Tom had been pretending to be single. Newspaper interviews had told you so, the radio had reaffirmed it, the TV also. But many people who knew Tom began writing to the media saying, 'Wait a minute here, Tom Jones is married and his wife and son live in Treforest.'

To Linda and Tom it was a great relief that the secret came out. Linda had been to join Tom in London to do a bit of flat hunting but the only mention she got was that she was his girlfriend. The pressure had been a bit much and now it was out for everyone to see — Tom Jones was married to Linda and had a little son called Mark. Linda said at the time, 'When the news of our marriage broke out I was very glad indeed. It was a great relief because I found it very difficult to keep the secret. I am glad all that business is over and done with.'

Tom also was highly relieved. 'All the time I was thinking of Linda and Mark and wondering how they would feel when they read what I said in interviews. I was convinced that sooner or later the secret would leak out. After all my friends in Wales knew I had a wife and child. It really did seem silly to go on with the deception. Like Linda, I too am glad that our marriage is no longer something kept in the background.'

When little Mark was told the secret was over he said, 'I'm glad everybody knows Tom Jones is my daddy. After the success of 'It's Not Unusual' Tom arrived back in Treforest as a hero and there was only one thing to do — celebrate. Tom, family and friends headed to The Wheatsheaf followed by hundreds of reporters from all over the world. Jack and Joan Lister, the owners, had never seen anything like it. The place was bursting at the seams with people demanding drink. The Listers came to an agreement: 'let them take over, let them have the pub.' Soon Tom's friends and relatives were pulling pints as the numerous cameras snapped Britain's biggest singing sensation.

Fame was wonderful but it did have its drawbacks. Tom realized that things could never ever be the same again. When he went to put his head down at 3 Cliff Terrace he was interrupted by a steady stream of fans to the front door armed with presents and requesting autographs. When they were not able to see him the fans would climb the high wall at the back of the garden. Others painted bricks with the message 'We love you, Tom' and left them outside the front door. It was the first local example of Tom-mania.

Tom may have been a big shot to his fans but to his parents he was still their boy — Tommy Woodward — and they always gave advice when they thought he needed it. Tom might have seemed a bit too big headed with his fancy clothes and car but Mother Freda was never long in putting him in his place. She told him, 'Listen Tommy boy, you may be a big shot up in London but down in Pontypridd you wipe your shoes when you come in, you're good to your wife and take your turn bringing in the coal.'

The one thing that niggled Tom was that although he had fame and money rolling in, his dad was still working down the pit and had the beginnings of a bad chest. Tom's mother was cutting sandwiches on a Sunday night for his dad to take on the night shift. Tom's conscience troubled him. Here he was sitting on thousands of pounds and driving a Jaguar and yet he was allowing his poor old dad to graft down the mine. He said to him, 'Dad, give it up, you don't have to work anymore.' But his father was a proud man and was not convinced that Tom would have enough money to be able to keep him and his mother for the rest of their lives.

He turned to Tom and said, 'Son, if I don't go into work tonight, I won't go for the rest of the week.' Off he went leaving Tom to try and convince his mother that he should leave the mine for ever.

Next on the agenda was accommodation. Tom and Linda had secured a flat in London but with the money rolling in from the disc and gigs, Tom decided to buy a house costing £7,000 in Manny Gate Lane, Shepperton. 'Put your money in bricks and mortar and you can't go wrong,' Mills advised him. Reporters had asked him if he was prepared to stay in Wales but he said, 'I don't relish the thought of leaving Wales but it is something that must be done. It would not be possible for me to live here and organize my career properly.' The Mills magic had worked so far, but what next? Britain had been conquered so there was only one other place to go — America. Mills realized that if Tom could conquer the USA and its vast market, what they were earning now would seem like peanuts.

America was the logical move, and the sooner the better. Since the apparent decline of Elvis and his jaunt into dull movies there were millions of women throughout the USA who yearned for a new sex symbol hero. Perhaps Tom, with his tight trousers and gyrating hips, was the man to fill the gap.

Gordon Mills got on the phone to showbiz agents in America and said that Tom was the hottest thing in Britain for years and destined to be as big, or even bigger, than Elvis. The agents were impressed especially when Gordon pointed out the huge British success of 'It's Not Unusual'. The patter merchant from Tonypandy had them all going and within a matter of weeks he had set up Tom's first US tour, and more importantly appearances on the highly rated Ed Sullivan Show.

Tom's American adventure coincided with the release of 'It's Not Unusual' over there, and like in Britain it began to make an impression on the charts. Tom was to make a series of five appearances on the Ed Sullivan Show, worth in all more than £10, 000. The Beatles had made their name on the show so why not Tom? He and Gordon flew out to America on 29 April 1965 to do the first and promote 'It's Not

Unusual'. It was Tom's first taste of American TV but he handled it well. Tom opened and closed the programme and his act stirred the emotions and fantasies of millions of women all over America. The female viewing audience had one complaint though — they said they would have liked to see more of Tom's body. The producers of the show put Tom in the same boat as Elvis. They thought the way he moved his pelvis was a bit too obscene for family TV so the orders went out to the cameramen to focus on the top part of Tom's body. One worried producer was heard to say, 'This guy looks as though he's making love to fresh air'. Tom was also given his orders. He said, 'It was really funny. When I went on the Ed Sullivan Show in New York the producers said, "Keep it cool, move sideways only, otherwise we'll black you out." 'Still, a censored Tom was better than no Tom at all and the excitable American females liked what parts they saw of him. The switchboard received hundreds of calls asking about this strange young man from Wales. The US critics also seemed to like Tom. They asked in headlines all over the country, 'Could this be the man to take over the crown from a now subdued Elvis?' Tom gave interviews all over the USA plugging 'It's Not Unusual'. When the Americans saw Tom on TV they were in for a big shock in more ways than one. When they heard his single they thought it must be a black man from the Deep South. But when they switched on Ed Sullivan there he was — a white man from South Wales. Meanwhile back in Britain Tom's first album — 'Along Came Jones' — was released in May 1965. The songs included 'I've Got A Heart', 'It Takes A Worried Man', 'Skye

Boat Song', 'Once Upon A Time', 'Memphis Tennessee', 'Whatcha Gonna Do', 'I Need Your Loving', 'It's Not Unusual', 'Autumn Leaves', 'The Rose', 'If You Need Me', 'Some Other Guy', 'Endlessly', 'It's Just A Matter Of Time', 'Spanish Harlem' and 'When The World Was Beautiful'.

From this album it was decided that Tom release 'With These Hands' as a follow up to 'It's Not Unusual'. But both Tom and Gordon were in for a set-back. Tom had done some demo tapes for independent record producer Joe Meek back in 1963, 'Little Lonely One' and 'That's What Love Will Do'. In the music business Meek had been considered rather eccentric. At one time in his career as an independent disc producer, he had set up a 'studio' in his small London flat and encouraged groups to record in his bathroom. He claimed the echo there made the music sound more commercial. But eccentric or not, Meek had persevered over the years and managed to find gold by producing one of the biggest selling discs of the decade — 'Telstar' by the Tornadoes. That record had sold more than five million copies and Meek was on the lookout for his next success. He was not slow to make a fast buck and when he saw Tom's star beginning to shine he remembered that he had kept the demo tapes Tom had made with the Senators. Through the Parlophone label he released the tracks 'Little Lonely One' and 'That's What Love Will Do'. When Tom and Gordon heard the news they could have throttled Meek. They saw it as a below-the-belt move which would only undermine their growing success and prosperity. To add insult to injury Meek had once made a homosexual pass on Tom when he was recording. Tom vented his anger to the newspapers. He encouraged people not to buy this rogue single' which was intended to jump on the bandwagon of his success. He said the single was dated and would only confuse the general public. 'We did them when we were Tommy Scott and the Senators, when we were not up to our present standard.' Meek hit back at the criticism in the media saying there was nothing wrong with the record and Tom should be proud of it. But in the end Tom's anger and antipathy won. He shunned any mention of 'Little Lonely One' and it nose-dived into obscurity. Tom returned to America to do a tour during July and August of 1965. He and Gordon saw it as the inevitable bread and butter work which was essential to get him known in this vast continent.

He was also due to make more appearances on the Ed Sullivan Show promoting his new US single, 'What's New Pussycat?'.

To say that Tom did not like 'What's New Pussycat?' would be an understatement. Burt Bacharach had written it for a film of the same title and when Tom heard it he gave it the thumbs down, saying it was just not him. He complained to Gordon saying it sounded like a 'Humpty Dumpty song'. But Gordon put his foot down. He told Tom that although he did not like the song he had to record it as it would be good for his career: it was riding on the back of a successful movie and destined to be a hit. Tom recalled later, 'I couldn't see it . . . my attitude wasn't wide open enough then to see that it could be a direct contrast and a breakthrough. Gordon persuaded me it would be a hit and he was right. I thought it would be a miss.' Reluctantly he went into the recording studios and sang the best he could to give it some 'feel'. Burt Bacharach personally produced 'What's New Pussycat?' and Tom admitted, 'He had me singing better than I'd ever done before. If Tom was to be the Great Pretender to Elvis the King's throne he had to at least show he was mixing in the same league, and what better than to meet the great man himself? To get Jones and Presley pictured together would be a great coup for the Mills publicity machine. Elvis was making a movie at the Panama Film Studios in Hollywood and a brief meeting was arranged. Tom went along and watched Presley in action in front of the cameras. Presley appeared a bit nervous at Tom's presence so his manager, Col Tom Parker, halted shooting and introduced both men. The meeting lasted only a few minutes but the effect was just right. Tom and Elvis had a chat and Tom was overjoyed that his big hero had heard some of his recordings. Elvis had become aware of this upstart British pretender. Tom later said, 'He was aware of what I was doing and knew that I had three records out and one album at the time. He knew most of the tracks on the album, which surprised me. He even had a copy of my recording of 'With These Hands', which he liked.

Tom was certainly stars truck during and after the meeting, but it had served the Mills purpose. It had built up Tom's image in America, boosted his confidence, and was further proof that anything was possible in the so-called land of free enterprise.

But if that was the glamour, there was another side to the story: hard work and plenty of it. Tom was not totally convinced that all the hard work was worth it. It was the heady days of 1965 and he joined the Dick Clark Caravan Tour with Sonny and Cher, the Turtles, Ronnie Dove, the Shirelles and Mel Carter. Travelling by bus up and down this vast country soon took its toll on Tom. And there were certain parts of American culture he disliked intensely. On a visit to the Deep South, infamous for the Ku Klux Klan and racial hatred, Tom and several black artistes stopped off for a meal at a café. A bunch of rednecks came in and started shouting and bawling as to why 'niggers' had been allowed in the place. The black guys were shaking partly with anger and partly with fear, and Tom told them to stay cool. After more taunts of 'nigger' one black fellow lost his temper and had a go at the rednecks. With chairs and bottles flying everywhere the law were soon on the scene and arrested the black man. As they were taking him to the paddy wagon Tom tried to put on a posh English accent and shouted, 'How dare you throw that man in there. Let him go at once.' A cop grabbed him and said menacingly, 'Are you going to keep out of this, boy?' Tom was quick to reply, 'Yes, sir', as they dragged the black man away. Tom commented, 'There was nothing I could do. They would have shot me. I don't think I'd ever come so close to death before. When you see the gun coming out of the holster and pointing at you...phew, I thought it was all over. That was my first taste of racial discrimination in the States'

The young Tommy Woodward in Pontypridd had had a few skirmishes as a Teddy Boy but nothing like this. When it came to facing the police in America this was a different ball game. Besides he could not risk his life during an obscure argument with an angry American policeman. Although he was willing to stand up against social injustice and racism, the odds were heavily against him. A copper in Ponty might give you a clip around the ear for being naughty, but he certainly would not shoot you. It was one of the first lessons Tom was to learn in America, a policeman, especially armed with a gun, was not someone you should argue with, even if you are in the right

Tom got back to England disillusioned and disheartened after a tour he described as 'murder, just no fun'. 'Sometimes we would do one date and then jump on the bus and it was so far to the next place we would get there and do the show and there wouldn't be the time to book into a hotel anywhere. 'Tom's frequent visits to America gave him an education into the high life of being a star. Gordon had always been one for the good life and he planned to enjoy success and the money that came with it. He and Tom went into a restaurant and Gordon ordered the most expensive caviar. Tom looked at the price and shouted, 'You're not going to eat that, are you? Look at the bloody price of it.' Gordon reassured him they could afford it. Tom admitted later, 'It took me a while to get used to it.' Back home in Wales they could live for a week on that sort of money.

On his return, after more than two months away, Tom told the media that he much preferred Britain as it was a much smaller country and he was more the centre of attention. He said the live work in America had been 'too hard going' but he was impressed with the following he had managed to build up. 'The Americans are crazy on British pop stars. The thing over there is to be British just as it is the reverse in Britain.'

1965 had certainly been a great year for Tom and Gordon and to cap it off beautifully Tom came fifth in the Melody Maker singer category. This was seen as a great achievement as he was only beaten by people such as John Lennon, Donovan, Cliff Richard and Mick Jagger. Tom was the top entry of the 'new faces' defeating fellow newcomers like Billy Fury and Eric Burdon of The Animals.

'It's Not Unusual' also appeared in the popularity charts as one of the best singles of the year and Tom was given the accolade of being 'the brightest hope for 1966'.

By the end of 1965 Tom could not believe his rampant success story and even had nightmares of being back at the beginning. In one he found himself back at the paper mills in Treforest saying to himself, 'What am I doing here? I'm Tom Jones, see. I'm rich.' But in the dream he's standing in his stage clothes beside a machine and can't escape. Waking up in a cold sweat soon brought him back to the reality of his success.

In another nightmare he dreamt he had lost his voice. He said at the time, 'Lately I keep feeling I'll wake up one morning and find it has gone. It's a natural fear I suppose because my voice has given me almost all I have in life.'

Pictures (1) Tom onstage 1980s (2) Having a pint between shows. (3) With wife Linda 1965 (4) Belting out the hits.

4. The Green, Green Grass of Home

The first year is said to be the most crucial in the pop business. Pop stars are made and broken according to the wishes of finicky fans. Gordon and Tom were delighted with their success in 1965 but saw 1966 as just as important and a consolidation period. To appease the growing demand of fans the singles 'This and That' and 'Stop Breaking My Heart' were released but they did not do well in the overall pop market. Perhaps Gordon and Tom had other things on their minds. They were inundated with live work which was very lucrative. Gordon and Tom realized that the volatility of the pop business could mean 'in' one minute and 'out' the next, so the wise thing to do was cash-in. So Tom sang his heart out to audiences in clubs and theatres up and down the country and the money flowed in.

With his success came a growing feeling that he was public property and was being watched all the time. Even going for a pint to his beloved Wheatsheaf was not to be the same anymore. 'Going back to Pontypridd isn't as easy as it sounds,' he said. 'There's nothing I'd like better than to be able to sit down with my mates in my local here, just have a drink and play cards, but that's in the past.

'It's part of my past that's gone no matter how much I try to recapture it. If I go into the same pub now they either think, "Who's that flash Harry throwing his money around?" or if I don't buy everyone in sight a pint I'm called a mean skinflint. How can a man win? It's not me that's changed, you know, that's the funny thing. It's Ponty that's changed towards me.'

During 1966 Tom was offered the chance to record the theme song from the new James Bond movie Thunderball. The song could never have been described as great but it managed to get Tom known on the worldwide market and the fact that it failed to do well in the pop charts did not worry Tom or Gordon. They saw the Bond song as merely another publicity vehicle. If America had provided the big experience of 1965, Australia was to provide the big experience of 1966. Tom and Gordon saw the Australian tour as an exciting adventure. If record sales were not going too well in Britain places such as Australia with a potentially vast record market could well come in handy. Tom and the Squires flew out for a five week tour joining another popular British band, Herman's Hermits.

Tom had experienced racial discrimination by police in the USA and was to experience other odd moments with the police in Australia. Newspapers reported that on one occasion police threatened to close his show in Sydney because he took his shirt off and began to move in 'a suggestive way'. When asked why he had taken his shirt off Tom said simply, 'Because it was too hot.'

It seems the Australian police were none too enamoured with Tom. In Brisbane a policeman walked into Tom's dressing room, poked him in the chest, and shouted, 'Now listen you. This is a clean town and it's gonna stay clean. Any trouble from you and we'll shove you inside. Okay?'

Tom said later, 'I felt like butting him with my nut but my hair had just been combed ready for the act.' During the Australian tour the dry arid heat seemed to affect Tom's voice and it was noticeable during some concerts that all was not well with his singing. When they got back to Britain Tom complained of a soreness in his throat. It couldn't have come at a worse time. Tom's singles were doing nothing and there were a lot of engagements to get through to keep the money flowing in. A bad throat could set their plans back years. A worried Gordon arranged for him to see a specialist and after a lengthy examination he concluded that Tom's tonsils had had such a battering they would have to come out.

To ordinary people having your tonsils out is no great deal but if your life depends on singing, it can be a make or break affair. One year of singing success and now he was to have his tonsils out. Tom's insecurity and nightmares increased.

He was admitted to the exclusive London Clinic on the Monday. The operation the following morning took about half an hour and even during it the clinic took hundreds of calls from fans, the more fanatical pleading to get hold of Tom's tonsils. Later, rumours abounded that the staff had put them in a jar and stored them for posterity. Among his hundreds of get-well letters was one from a woman aged seventy-four.

The episode was more a nuisance than anything else, causing him to cancel two important engagements. He had been asked by Burt Bacharach to go to an Academy Award dinner in Hollywood where 'What's New, Pussycat?' had been nominated for a prize; the other date was the Variety Club of Great Britain luncheon at which the Duke of Edinburgh was to be guest of honour.

Although the operation was a success, the surgeons had noticed bruising on the vocal chords and insisted on Tom giving his voice a complete rest. It had taken a battering over the years. When he was told to avoid cigarettes and alcohol Gordon saw the ideal chance to help reshape Tom's habits.

Tom recalled years later, 'I always smoked Woodbines and drank beer. My manager said that one day I'd be smoking cigars and drinking champagne. I said, "I love Woodbines and I love beer, and that's that." So what am I doing today? Drinking champagne and smoking expensive cigars. Times change. You change.'

When Tom was able to sing again everyone was relieved that it had not affected his incredible voice. His first post-operation gig was on the pop TV programme Ready Steady Go. Afterwards he joined female singer Dusty Springfield, pop group the Mindbenders and comedian Roy Castle at the Blackpool Opera House. Further TV spots were lined up throughout Europe and another stint in America was on the cards.

Tom was not long back on the road when he literally came off the road. During the summer he was driving some friends home in his brand new red Jaguar in the early hours of the morning, when it skidded and came off the road crashing into some railings. He was lucky to escape with no worse than a few stitches over his left eye.

So far, 1966 had been a difficult year and it appeared the hits were drying up. But Gordon and Tom were not really that worried. They saw themselves as playing for time and concentrating on Tom being a live, rather than recording act. The disc 'Once There Was a Time' with 'Not Responsible' on the other side was making a ripple in the charts, so why not be happy with that for the time being? When asked about his downward turn in hit discs Tom replied that it was very difficult getting the right material.

He and Gordon had sifted through hundreds of songs but still had not come up with the magic formula to emulate the success of 'It's Not Unusual'. If anything, the critics made it seem worse. They slagged off 'Once There Was a Time' and although annoyed, Tom and Gordon shrugged it off. If the hit records weren't fast in coming, acting offers certainly were. Tom was sounded out by Hollywood. Producer Joe Pasternak wanted him to have a go at making westerns and Paramount produced a provisional contract with an offer to work with actress Ann-Margret.

The problem was that in true US style they wanted Tom to drop everything and start as soon as possible which, because of future engagements, would have been financial suicide.
From his days as a youngster at the White Palace Cinema in Pontypridd, Tom had had a secret

yearning to play a cowboy. Gordon was quick to point out that apart from the financial consequences Tom had a Welsh accent and no acting experience. Too many potential stars had gone to America to make a movie only to find it being done on a shoestring with a poor script. Gordon was too shrewd to let Tom fall into that trap. He advised Tom it was too early to make a move in that direction.

Although Tom had made a dismal showing in the charts during 1966 his reputation and standing was in no doubt. In the Melody Maker poll published in September 1966 he was voted top British male singer, knocking Cliff Richard off his perch. The other major music paper the New Musical Express voted him the second best male singer in Britain (after Cliff) and fifth in the world section.

All year Tom and Gordon had been searching for the elusive hit that would equal 'It's Not Unusual' and put them back into the charts. All they needed was a bit of luck to find the right song but so far it had eluded them. Tom was to find this luck after listening to his hero Jerry Lee Lewis.

He always maintained that Jerry Lee was his greatest rock and roll influence. On a visit to New York Tom bought Jerry Lee's 'Country Songs for City Folks' and on that album was the song 'The Green, Green Grass of Home'. When Tom heard it he just knew it was right. It reminded him of his ties with Wales and how sometimes he got homesick for the old days in Treforest. Perhaps this song more than any other is instantly recognizable as the Jones song. 'The old home town looks the same as I step down from the train and there to meet me is my mamma and papa; Down the road I look and there runs Mary, hair of gold and lips like cherries, it's good to touch the Green, Green Grass of Home. 'Although the song was American it sounded strangely like an old Welsh song. Tom could feel the sentiment in his bones and was sure it would be a success. He recorded the song and even let Jerry Lee Lewis hear it and got his seal of approval. 'The Green, Green Grass of Home' was released in December 1966 and went straight into the top twenty. It swept through Britain like a fever, spending seven weeks at the number one spot, fending off groups such as The Beach Boys, Manfred Mann and The Kinks, and a total of twenty-two weeks in the charts. At the end of the year Tom Jones was riding high again. When 'The Green, Green Grass of Home' was released in America Tom won over a very important fan — Elvis Presley himself. Elvis was on a coach with his entourage when he heard Tom singing it on the radio. They had all been touring and were feeling very homesick for Memphis. When the tones of 'The Green, Green Grass of Home' came over the radio Elvis and his boys broke down and cried. He got one of his 'Memphis Mafia' to phone the local radio station and play it again and the overwhelmed disc jockey played it four times. Elvis later recalled in an interview: 'We just sat in the bus crying. Tom singing 'The Green, Green Grass of Home' reminded us of being back home.' If there was one person who basked in Tom's success more than anyone it was

Gordon Mills, and deservedly so. Mills had brought Tom from the obscurity of singing in a valley club to being one of the most successful singers in the world. He had moulded Tom from what he regarded as an uncut diamond to a highly polished, sophisticated, medallion man. In the matter of a few years Mills had completely changed Tom's image.

After Tom came back from the first American tour Gordon realized perhaps they were trying for the wrong sort of market. Teenage audiences were all right but had little economic spending power. More mature audiences, with their larger spending power, might appreciate Tom better, he thought. Gordon Mills said, 'Tom was so strong, too strong on stage, that kids were afraid of him. This is when I thought of trying him with a mature audience.' The plan worked. Gordon steered Tom away from the teenybopper gigs to the more sophisticated nightclub and theatre circuit. Out went the blousy shirt and on came the tuxedo. Mature adults need their heroes too and the result astounded both Tom and Gordon. So-called mature people began to act like teenyboppers when they saw Tom. Tom was amazed at the effect of his new image. 'What you would expect in a ballroom with teenagers started to happen in these nightclubs with mature people. Women started to go crazy and back then it was completely different because it had never happened before.'

If one medallion man could make it, well so could another. Gordon's old friend Gerry Dorsey had been asking him to take over his career and turn him into a success. Gordon believed he had the success formula tied up. He had changed Tom's showbiz name from Tommy Scott to Tom Jones after a hit movie of the day and a Henry Fielding character, so why not do the same with Dorsey? Unusual names always fired the imagination of the public and what better than the crazy name of Engelbert Humperdinck? It took a year for Gordon to get round to managing Dorsey but when he did he told him, 'I'm ready to take you under my wing but first you must change your name. Gerry Dorsey is too easy to forget. Engelbert Humperdinck can be confused, mispronounced or misspelled, but it's a name that no one will ever forget.' He explained that he had come across the name after looking through a pile of classical records and saw the name Engelbert Humperdinck, an obscure composer who wrote the music for Hansel and Gretel. It took Dorsey three weeks to learn how to pronounce his new name. His wife Pat did not think much of his new 'handle' and neither did he, but they relied on Gordon's imagination hoping it would be a good bet. Dorsey would confess to friends, 'I only hope Gordon knows what he is doing. If it goes wrong it could finish me as a singer. 'By the beginning of 1966 Gerry Dorsey the struggling singer was forgotten. In came the new image and sophistication of Engelbert Humperdinck. Engel said at the time, 'It's been a little hard to adjust to. All my life I had a simple name and all of a sudden I've got a monster of a thing to sign and pronounce. Humperdinck was to fit into the medallion man image. He was to appeal to mature middle-aged women. This embryo sex-symbol was to be more 'ballady' and middle of the road than Tom — who was more rock and soul orientated. The singers' images did not clash. If Tom's act was wild then Engel's act was cool. If Tom's act was raunchy Engel's act was gentle.

With the name and tuxedo attached, Engelbert was unleashed onto the world via an obscure international song contest in Knokke le Zoutte in Belgium. He was a member of the English team which included Eden Kane, Jimmy Wilson, Truly Smith and Chloe Walters. The team won but although his singing had not greatly impressed the critics, the reporters at the event certainly thought his name struck a chord and soon stories began to appear about this mysterious new singer. The Mills publicity team went to town. Contacts that had been built up through the promotion of Tom were used to Engelbert's advantage. Gordon played Engelbert singing his own composition 'Stay' to producers at Decca Records. They liked it, but it was the name that grabbed their attention. To the music moguls this man with the unusual name was a million miles away from Gerry Dorsey. Gordon secured a recording contract releasing both 'Stay' and another singled called 'Dommage, Dommage.' The first single made a slight ripple and 'Dommage, Dommage' sold quite well in Europe. But a great song was needed to catapult Engel into the hearts of the female millions. Gordon was driving along the road one day when he heard an old American country and blues song on the radio. The tune agreed with him, it was catchy and romantic. But after hearing it he could not remember what it was called. By luck, the next night, the song was played on radio again and Gordon contacted the music publisher.

The song was called 'Release Me' and Gordon was sure this would be the perfect song for Humperdinck. It was to be a lucky time for both men. Gordon heard that British singer Dickie Valentine was ill with flu and had to drop out of the bill on Sunday Night At The London Palladium — a live TV show watched by millions of viewers.

Gordon contacted the show's musical director, Val Parnell, and convinced him Engel should have the Valentine spot. Engel sang 'Release Me' and the next day the single began selling in its thousands. It swamped the British charts, eventually making it to number one and selling a million copies. It remained at the top for five weeks and sold a total of 5,000,000 copies worldwide. Engelbert now refused any recognition of his old name. To him Gerry Dorsey had been a failure and was now firmly buried in the past. He refused to answer letters addressed to Gerry Dorsey and would not answer people if they addressed him by that name. Some music critics thought Gordon was cutting his own throat by having two singers in his stable aiming for the same sort of market. But Gordon had it worked out — there was plenty of room for both and besides, more logically, two successful singers meant double the profit. Tom was to be 'Mr Sex' and Engel 'Mr Romance'. Gordon had successfully created two medallion men and said there might even be room for another one in the stable if the right singer and image came along.

Gordon not only had a tremendous business brain but also a certain amount of boyish charm that helped him dominate the middle of the road music industry during the 1960s. But he had a ruthless side as well. When Tom was booked to appear on a radio pop programme the producer informed them that Tom would do his spot halfway through the show. Gordon lost his rag and tore into him. 'You've got the greatest singer in the world and you dare to put him in the middle of the show. Either he closes the show or we go.' Needless to say the producer was taken aback and Tom closed the show. Gordon would defend Tom to such an extent that at times it became an obsession with him.

Johnny Bennett rang Gordon with what he thought was interesting information. 'I've just heard a cracking singer. His name's Tony Christie.' Gordon said, 'What sort of singer is he? How would you compare him to Tom?' Johnny replied, 'Oh, you can't compare him with Tom. But he's thinner than Tom and his voice, range wise, is up there at the top.' Mills replied, 'Bollocks', and hung up the phone.
Christie later became a star in his own right recording such hits as 'Hey Las Vegas' and 'I Did What 1 Did for Maria'. Meanwhile Tom cruised along the pop scene recording another Jerry Lee Lewis number called 'Detroit City'. He had bookings all over the world and starred at sell-out concerts.

On one occasion at the Talk of the Town, London, Hollywood legend and ex-wife of Frank Sinatra, Ava Gardner, walked into Tom's dressing room after the show. She told him she had seen his show four times and saw Tom as the natural successor to Sinatra. 'He's got the same kind of guts and grit that

Frank had,' she told reporters. She left Tom her phone number just in case they 'ever had the opportunity of filming together.'

During all this time Tom had never forgotten his vow to take his father out of the pits forever and give him and his mother a better life. One day Tom's father received a phone call from his son's financial advisers assuring him that he could retire from the pit with no worries about money. Tom said, 'The only way I finally convinced him was when I asked him how much he would earn until his planned retirement at sixty-five. He didn't know off hand but I said, "We'll work it out and I'll give you that amount of money to stop work". The next thing was to move his parents to be near him. Tom moved out of his home, Rose Bank, at Manny Gate Lane, Shepperton, into Springfield House, Sunbury-on-Thames. The new house cost more than £25,000, considered a fortune in those days, and had five bedrooms, two bathrooms, a lounge and sitting-rooms which were soon to be stocked with expensive antique furniture. Tom gave the house in Shepperton to his parents as a present and bought them a white Granada so that they could travel back to Wales when they wanted to. Tom's father was fifty-six when he first learned to drive a car but Tom encouraged him to drive his Rolls-Royce and Mercedes too, especially when he was off on tour: 'You can help keep them in trim, Dad.' At first Tom's parents missed their old way of life in Treforest and it took some time for them to settle. Tom's father said at the time, 'I find all this free time a big difference from life down the pits. I was up every morning for the better part of my life, never seeing daylight, as I worked underground for my wage packet. You have to adjust to things after all that time. 'You need time to get things in the right light. I had a lucky life, I must admit, and never an accident in all my time as a miner, though I've seen my mates in terrible ones. You didn't have time to worry though. If you had you'd never have gone on would you? 'One thing that Tom's dad missed about South Wales was the beer. He had to get used to a new brand but soon settled down to supping it and was a regular down at his new English local most days. When Tom had the time he would join him for a pint. A night at the pub with his father was a great enjoyment for Tom. It meant he was still close to his family and was never homesick for his roots in Treforest. It was as though a little part of Wales had moved to England to be with him. When asked if she ever missed being back home his mother said, 'Ponty? No, I don't think I've ever had any regrets about moving here. It was a good home to us but now we've got new roots and I think you must adapt to fit your surroundings.'

Freda and Tom Snr said they were happy because they not only had Tom nearby but had all their familiar bits and pieces around them from back home. They even brought the bed Tom was born in to the luxury of their new house. Although by 1967 Tom's image was geared more to a mature audience he still had a lot of support from the younger generation. In the New Musical Express annual pop poll he came top in the UK male singer section, Cliff Richard came second and surprise, surprise, Mills' other medallion man Engelbert Humperdinck came in third. In the world section Tom came second after Elvis Presley. The Jones magic was still going great guns but one thing bothered him — his nose. Tom's nose had borne the brunt of many fights back in the days when he was a Teddy boy in Pontypridd. The voice was there, the tuxedo was there, the movements were there, but the nose . . well it didn't exactly fit in with the superstar image. Gordon agreed something would have to be done about it. Sometimes the old nose looked bad in pictures and that wasn't on for a sex symbol. The overall plan was to make Tom even more attractive to his growing number of mature female fans, but if you are a macho superstar you can't just tell the world you're having a nose job, it just doesn't sound right, so an excuse for entering hospital had to be made up. Accordingly the media were told that Tom was having an operation for 'some sinus trouble'.

When Tom and the new nose appeared the media became rather . . .nosy. The change was noticeable straight away. Gone was the protruding beak and in its place was a small film star's nozzle. To put them off the scent (to pardon the pun) Tom told newspapermen he had noticed the nose was shorter and this was because the doctors had cut 'something out of it'. Gordon and Tom agreed that it had been a good move. The next beauty spot that had to be sorted out was Tom's teeth. To put it mildly they had never looked attractive and were decaying rather badly. So for a few quid more Tom had them capped. He said later that it was a good investment as he had to look attractive and presentable to the greatest number of people. He pointed out that in the cruel world of pop you can't afford to have anything ugly about yourself. Perhaps he also had the competition of Engelbert in mind.

So the new-look 'pretty boy' Tom was ready for his first appearance in front of the Queen in the Royal Variety Performance at the London Palladium. Playing the Royal Variety Performance was a petrifying experience. Performing in front of the Queen is a nerve-racking task for most stars. Beatle John Lennon, during a previous Royal Variety Performance, covered up his nerves by saying 'Those in the cheap seats, clap your hands. The rest of you can rattle your jewellery.' Before the show it was not only Tom who felt butterflies flutter in his stomach. He just had to look at seasoned performers like Norman Wisdom, Des O'Connor, Dusty Springfield and Tommy Cooper to know that it was no easy feat. Tom was terrified and during his short appearance when he sang 'It's Not Unusual' and two other songs, his top lip stuck to his teeth. But even if he was highly nervous it did not really show through. He went down a storm and the Queen was said to be highly amused with the energetic hip movements. After the show she asked Tom what he thought of America and he said he liked performing there. The Queen replied, 'Good, they are nice people aren't they?' Tom agreed. She asked Tom how he kept so fit. 'By getting eight hours sleep a night, Your Majesty,' the Woodward boy replied with a grin.

5. Why, Why, Why, Delilah?

The year of 1968 was a further period of consolidation. Tom's charisma was flying to heights never known before and then came another big seller — 'I'm Coming Home' — also written by Les Reed, the man behind 'It's Not Unusual'. Tom had gigs all over the country. The film offers still came in but he was still hesitant about taking any of them up. He had a full schedule and any free time was precious indeed.

He was so busy he confessed to the media that sometimes on tour he was bewildered as to where he was. Another town, another stage, another audience, another few grand in the bank.

In America he did a tour of the cabaret circuit and took the Flamingo Hotel in Las Vegas by storm. Stars such as Tony Bennett, Frank Sinatra, Dean Martin, and Judy Garland dropped into see what this hip-swivelling sensation was all about and they were impressed. So successful was his gig at Las Vegas that a live album was released the next year called 'Live at the Flamingo' which captured the early magic of the man. Gordon saw the tour as a golden opportunity to wheel and deal with the American media and music moguls to set up more lucrative deals for the following year. Meanwhile success followed success. If 'It's Not Unusual', 'The Green, Green Grass of Home', and 'I'm Coming Home' were giant sellers, then the haunting lyrics of a song called 'Delilah' were to catapult it into the same selling league.

In many ways 'Delilah' was to be the icing on the cake for Tom's rapid success in recent years. If anything it was the most powerful of his songs. It was the violent story of a man's revenge on his girlfriend for being unfaithful. Some critics lambasted it, saying its content was too violent. In America the song took off like a rocket; the whole feeling of the song seemed to sum up the way American society was going. The American censors were particularly attentive when Tom was due to make another appearance on the Ed Sullivan Show singing 'Delilah'. Much to Tom's amazement they came up with the ultimatum that the lyrics had to be changed for the show. They made him change the second verse where it says, 'At break of day when the man drove away' to 'When the man was across the way'.

An astonished Tom said later, 'Murdering Delilah [as the song relates] was fine with them [the censors] but not the fact that he stayed with her all night.'

During 1968 in Britain, Tom did a series of concerts at Bournemouth, renting a house there and using it to entertain showbiz friends after each show. With his increasing fame the media had speculated that he had been seen out with a variety of women including model Joyce Ingalls, American singer Nancy Wilson and Mary Wilson of the Supremes, while Linda stayed at home. She was furious when she read in gossip column at home one day that Mary Wilson was staying at the Bournemouth house.

She was so angry she decided to head down to Bournemouth to check-out the story. When Linda arrived at the house Tom and his road manager, Chris Ellis, denied the story, but with her woman's intuition she looked around for any clue of another woman being there. She found a gourmet meal simmering in the oven, and said to Tom, 'That looks nice, Tommy. Did you cook it?' (She full well knew that Tom could not cook to save his life.) 'No,' Tom replied, 'Chris Ellis cooked it. Didn't I tell you? He's been taking lessons.' A close shave or an innocent explanation? No matter what, Linda had shown she was still a power to be reckoned with in their relationship, and Tom had a deep fear and respect for her which stretched back to their days as children playing in Laura Street. Like most valleys men, he at times was terrified of 'the missus'.

As Tom's worldwide popularity increased, Sir Lew Grade, controller of ATV, realized that he was big property and highly marketable, and after extensive negotiations agreed to sign him up for a series of TV shows which would show him to be 'the greatest singer in the world.'

It was a three year contract to do nearly eighty shows. This meant virtually locking himself away in the ATV Elstree Studios for six months of the year but the rewards were worth it. The contract was said to be worth around £9 million and Grade expected returns of more than £20 million from American sales alone. The prediction was proved to be more than right. By 1971 the show was showing in thirty-two countries which made Tom technically the highest paid singer in the world. If you look at these early shows you can see what the attraction was all about. Here was Tom giving it all, every show, week in week out, like some kind of demented sex machine and driving the women mad every time. Certainly by the time the show reached America Tom was the sex symbol to see.

At the beginning of 1969 Myron and Byron reared their heads again. This time it was not at one of Tom's concerts but at the High Court in London. Mr Brian Neil, acting on behalf of the two former managers Raymond Glastonbury and Raymond Godfrey, said his clients had a happy relationship with the pop star before Gordon Mills took over and the hit of 'It's Not Unusual' happened. The judge was asked to decide how much Myron and Byron were to receive from Tom. They claimed that under the contract they signed in 1964 Tom had made it clear they were to get five per cent of his earnings 'in perpetuity'. Tom and his lawyers claimed this was not the case and the two men were only entitled to five per cent of his earnings up to the time he became famous.

The case, involving thousands of pounds, was later settled between both parties. In 1969 — the year when all his professional dreams were to come true — Tom undertook a three month whistle-stop tour of the USA playing forty-one cities and earning a flat fee of £30,000 a week. In addition he was signed for a season at the Flamingo Club in Las Vegas for a top line fee of £350,000.

The Jones fever really started at the Copacabana Club in New York as thousands of screaming women besieged the place and Tom had to be put under a presidential style guard. In the following years he would be associated with ladies throwing their underwear at him, but how did it start? As he described it, 'It was at the Copacabana Club, I was sweating and ladies would hand me their cocktail napkins. One hurled her underwear. I was astounded.'

If one lady can take off her knickers then hundreds of others realized that they could as well, so the tradition started which American columnist Earl Wilson first witnessed and told a shocked pop world. When Tom would play the Copacabana the panties would rain down on the stage. This led one commentator to remark- 'There were so many panties thrown at Tom it looked like an explosion in a laundry'.

Outside in the New York streets hundreds of women of all ages and sizes chanted Tom's name, while inside they screamed and jumped on the tables. Others went further, vowing they would commit suicide and throw themselves off the club roof if Tom did not meet them and touch them. The local media agreed that there had been nothing like it since the early days of Frank Sinatra. Tom's fans clambered into scenes resembling rugby scrums.

They would fight over such things as used Kleenex tissues which he had wiped his head with.

If security had been tight it had to be tightened even further. Armed security guards surrounded him whenever he moved — both on stage and off stage. 'It's pretty frightening, you know, having a couple of men with revolvers walk you on stage but I suppose someone thinks it's necessary. I don't really want to be ripped to pieces,' Tom said at the time.

Whenever Tom appeared at the Copacabana Club something crazy was always bound to happen. One woman tried to pull Tom's hair out at the roots until a bouncer knocked her out of the way. Tom commented, 'A bit painful that. Ever had your hair pulled? She was clever enough, and deserved it.' Another mad fan ripped all the buttons off his waistcoat and took them home to show her relatives.

One night when Tom was performing on stage a blonde woman aged about twenty-five, dressed in a white silk trouser suit, decided she had to meet her hero at any costs. She worked out that the usual way to the stage was out of the question, so she leaped up on the tables, running across them until she got near the stage. The whole club was stunned and she got within a whisker of Tom before a security man put her over his shoulders and carried her out. In the foyer of the club she could be seen weeping with frustration. Tom said after the incident, 'It was a frightening minute, I can tell you. I could see her starting to come across the tables and what could I do about it? I thought I had had it. She looked pretty determined and was moving fast. I don't know what my singing was like. My mind was so distracted by what she would do if she reached me.'

On another occasion in the Copacabana a fan started to climb on stage and tried to grab Tom. One of the security guards pulled her back to her table and her boyfriend came at him with a knife. The security guard had to act fast and landed a punch on him knocking him out. Two other guards carried him out unconscious and the woman stayed on to see the show. All the crazy incidents and mass hysteria meant that at one point there were 100 security guards at each show. The trouble was not only confined to female fans. Some men got jealous of Tom and the attention he was getting from all these women. One bodyguard broke his knuckle when he punched a New York troublemaker on the right earhole. 'He came up looking for bother as Tom and I were going into our hotel,' he told the press.

Once, a group of Mafia thugs decided to invade Tom's dressing room but were swiftly dealt with by Tom's friend and 'minder' Chris Ellis, a slightly built man from Nantgarw, South Wales. He got them out by delivering a firm, four-letter farewell message.

At the Flamingo Hotel in Las Vegas it was the same story with sell-out houses and women crying outside because they could not get in. On opening night the management were besieged by offers of money, presents, and even personal favours to find fans seats.

Gordon Mills said at the time, 'This town has gone absolutely mad for Tom. If ever Wales and Britain should be proud of anyone it's Tom Jones because he's the biggest thing seen here for years.' Tom was playing to 1,000 people a night with more than 400 people being turned away during the first show. Tom put so much energy into turning on his audiences that he lost an average of six pounds in weight at each show.

What was it about American women? How come they were so over the top compared to their British counterparts? Tom tried to come up with an explanation: 'It might be that the American woman is a bit suppressed. Maybe she can't let her hair down enough with people like Perry Como or Andy Williams, but with me she can open up all the valves. Kids don't have these problems. But with the twenty to forty age bracket, older women need an outlet. '

All the major celebrities in town came to see him, but to one of them Tom's performance was just the stimulus he needed to give him the confidence to perform live again. Elvis Presley had lost a lot of his confidence as he had given up live work to make a series of uninspired movies and felt that his popularity was on the wane. He yearned for the old days when he could give it all to a live audience.

He began to hang around Vegas checking out the acts. When he saw Tom's act his eyes nearly bulged out of his head. Here was this young man with a tuxedo and Afro hairdo actually driving the females crazy with his sex appeal. Tom's trousers looked as though they had been sprayed on and the tightness of them left nothing to the imagination once those hips got moving. As the hips and the singing hypnotized the female audience, Elvis was astounded when respectable looking women rushed to the stage screaming and throwing their room keys to the singer. Some of them went even further and took off their panties and then threw them on to the stage. He realized Tom had made the transformation from stimulating teenyboppers to hypnotizing adult females with blatant sexuality.

In those days you could fairly describe the Flamingo as a madhouse. Full of screaming, panting, excitable women who wanted to rip off Tom's trousers and maul him under the bright lights. The Flamingo capitalized on this rampant fever. When customers sat down at their tables they found a little bottle filled with 'fever pills' and even local radio had reports of 'fever clinics' sprouting up all over Vegas. Then fever-hype snowballed. The place was inundated with women demanding tickets at any price. At one point it seemed the fever was getting out of control.

Elvis thought Tom's act rather lewd, but when he said this to his 'Memphis Mafia' they pointed out that he had done the same thing during his early days. Elvis denied ever being 'that vulgar'. But he was impressed with Tom. He said to friends, 'Tom is the only man who ever came close to the way I sing. He has that ballsy feeling.' Perhaps the fever also gripped Elvis because he went backstage to meet the pretender to his crown. Tom was extremely nervous when he heard that the King wanted to meet him . . . little Tommy Woodward from Laura Street, Treforest. At 3 a.m., The King entered the dressing room with Priscilla. Tom was speechless. He had an even bigger shock when Priscilla asked him for his autograph.

Tom said, 'Priscilla asked me for an autographed picture for their baby. The kid can hardly be six months old. Priscilla said it would be something she would treasure in the years to come so you can imagine how pleased I was to oblige. They are a really great couple, the Presleys. 'Without any fuss at all they came to the show and sat down right in front of the arena. Half way through my act I stopped and introduced him to the audience. All you could hear was clapping and cheering. Then when Elvis took a bow I said, ' 'OK, that's enough. Sit down". Everyone roared and laughed with them, and I carried on with my act.' Elvis told Tom he had joined in the standing ovation for him. Elvis was to say later, 'You know, it was seeing Tom on stage here in Vegas that gave me the urge to perform again.'

The two men got along together extremely well, and Elvis invited Tom to join him in Hawaii for a few days. Whilst they were there Elvis went out to buy each of them a guitar, and there followed a night which Tom later described as 'one I'll never forget as long as I live' as the superstars shared song after song, 'Blue Suede Shoes', 'Hound Dog' and all, in what must have been the greatest singsong of all time. But perhaps the shadow of what was to come was detectable when Elvis confessed that he was having trouble keeping his weight down and was resorting to 'medical measures' to help him. Tom urged him to look after himself and not rely on medication, in whatever form. Another world star to call on Tom was Betty Grable, number one pin up of the war years, who asked him for an autographed picture so she could hang it on her bedroom wall. Tom was overwhelmed once more. He said, 'I can hardly wait to tell my Dad about this, he'll be knocked out. He's been a fan of hers for years.' During the tour Tom bumped into another celebrity, Bobby Darin, and could not believe the change in the man. Darin was going through his hippy flower power phase. He had given up his tuxedo crooning image, had announced that he was to give up his possessions and demanded that he be called plain 'Bob'. He began to sing 'meaningful' songs in the vein of Bob Dylan and preached to the world about the shallowness of being a cabaret singer.

Bobby Darin walked into Tom's dressing room unshaven and dressed in denims, looking a million miles away from the smart Hollywood jet-setter who had captivated the world with his singing. Tom was taken aback at the sight, and when they talked Darin could have been from a different planet. He told Tom he had given up his flash lifestyle and travelling in limousines, and now had an old jeep. He could not identify with his past.

After this rather strange meeting Darin drove off in his old jeep, Tom in his limousine. Tom shook his head in bewilderment and said to his minder, 'I can't understand what gets into a man's head to swap a limousine for a jeep, change his whole attitude to life and want to put behind him all that's gone before him as an artiste.' Tom had no doubt which he enjoyed. He had been rich and had been poor, and he knew that being rich was far more enjoyable than living the life of Laura Street again.

By the end of the year Tom could easily have used the phrase *veni, vidi, vici:* I came, I saw, I conquered. By the time his gruelling American tour ended in November he had five LPs in the US charts Back in Britain Tom was booked to appear at the Royal Variety Performance for the second time, but this time he was heading the bill. With the vast experience he had gained in the USA, Tom's act was certainly more raunchy yet had a unique sophistication about it. Once again the posh audience were impressed and to the viewing millions who later saw his performance on television it was merely re-affirmation that here was the greatest singer in Britain, if not the world. After the show Tom was presented to the Queen and Prince Philip. The Prince, well known for being outspoken, said to Tom, 'What do you gargle with, pebbles?' Tom laughed it off and took it as part and parcel of the royal wit. The next day he was not so pleased. Prince Philip spoke at business lunch referring to Tom.

Not realizing that he was being reported, he said, 'Last night we went to the Royal Variety Performance. The last man to come on was Tom Jones. Now there is a young man of about twenty-five or something worth probably about £3m. It is very difficult to see how it is possible to become immensely valuable by singing what I think are most hideous songs. I would not say this about the Beatles." The place abounded with laughter and when the news got back Tom felt thoroughly humiliated. He exploded to his friends, 'I was giving my services to charity. What did he think it was — a bloody royal audition?' The media were quick to capitalize on the situation and Tom was asked what he thought about the Prince's cutting remarks. The newspapers expected fireworks but Tom, being a media veteran by this time and guided by Gordon Mills, constrained his temper until an acceptable version of his side of the events emerged. He said: 'I don't know what happened. The thing I was annoyed about was that the Prince ran down the whole show. It doesn't matter what he thinks about me, there are a lot of people who don't like my music. But the show is for charity. I wasn't doing an audition for the Duke. The show's got to be disjointed. You cannot look at the whole show because there are too many artistes on stage and it's not like television.'

Regarding the Prince's remarks about the money he was alleged to be earning Tom said, 'I pay a lot of taxes. I earn a lot of money for this country and I give my services to charity.' The media were looking for blood, though. What did he think of the Royal Family? Tom replied, 'If the country can afford them I think they are a good thing.' When asked if he wanted an apology from the Palace he said, 'No, not really.' Prince Philip was worried about the bad publicity and it troubled him to the extent that he ordered Buckingham Palace officials to write a letter to Tom disclaiming the remarks in apologetic terms.

Gordon and Tom were still angry but it was another sign that they had made it. What other singer could command an apology from the monarch's husband? None. The Jones fellow was in a league of his own. A year later, Tom did a special charity show for the World Wildlife Fund at the Talk of the Town. No fees were paid, but the artistes on the show were invited to a cocktail party at Buckingham Palace. As the drinks flowed, Prince Philip and the Queen eyed Tom nervously. Philip decided to cut the ice once and for all and walked straight over to Tom, looked into his eyes, and said, man to man, 'Look, I would like to set the record straight. I was misquoted. What l said was that you sing so hard you must gargle with pebbles. But I am not criticizing the sound. I just don't know how you do it.' Tom said after the meeting, 'He was supposed to have criticized the amount of money I was earning. He told me he wasn't criticizing me but that he was at a small businessmen's meeting — they were warning that they couldn't make enough money, that they couldn't survive, and he said, ' 'When somebody comes along like Tom Jones, when a man can make that sort of money, I don't see why you can't do it". He explained all that to me and I thought it was very nice. He didn't have to.'

Controversy involving people in such high places did more good than harm and Tom launched himself into the 1970s with a prestige never known before for any modern singing star. In Britain and America he topped the popularity polls to such an extent that the music critics were forced to concede, 'Who can stop the Jones boy?' It was to be the same story for the golden stable's other runner — Engelbert. Manipulating Engel's career had been like a game of chess for Mills.

He had played the game before with Tom and knew most of the best moves when it came to launching Engelbert onto the Las Vegas circuit. On the strength of Gordon's management of Tom Jones, coupled with a bit of cheek and cunning, Mills had arranged for Engel to start at the top in Vegas. He convinced the management of the Rivera Hotel that Engel was worth £35,000 to do a series of concerts there. The management were sceptical but Gordon assured them Engelbert would eventually be as big a draw as Tom and they were getting him cheap. The management thought that Mills knew something they didn't and gave Engel the booking. It was a gamble in the biggest gambling city in the world.

When he arrived in Las Vegas Engel was nervous of the challenge before him but the failure of the Dorsey days had gone. The very name — Engelbert Humperdinck— seemed to open doors for him and make him instantly popular. The American comedians joked about it, and the media were curious to the extent he got plenty of free publicity. After Engel had made only a few appearances at the hotel he was able to boast that the three week run had been fully booked. Two years later Mills was able to get Engel a contract there for almost half a million pounds. The Mills magic had worked yet again.

During 1969 the money had been rolling in not only for Tom but for Engelbert also. The big problem was that a huge chunk, hundreds of thousands of pounds, was heading into the coffers of the very alert and needy British taxman. Gordon, to put it in Welsh terms, nearly had his hair off and shouted to his accountants, 'Find us some way of paying less tax otherwise you're all finished.'

The answer came with the formation of a company called MAM. It sounded posh enough when you said it— Management and Agency Music — and three directors were Gordon Mills, Tom Jones and of course Engelbert Humperdinck. If the Jones and Humperdinck mania had confined itself to showbiz it was ready to spread into the financial world to their advantage. MAM launched itself onto the stock market at the low price of 13s 3d (66p) a share. Previously it had been the screaming females jumping onto the Jones—Humperdinck bandwagon, but now it was the equally hysterical money men of the city. To put it plainly, the shares were an astounding bargain. How could you go wrong with big money earners like Jones with his world-wide success and Humperdinck who put the romance back into every middle-aged broken heart?

Tom had 863,750 shares and they were worth an instant £573,233. By the end of the month after the launch of MAM, the value of the shares leapt up to an incredible £597,938. The company had another purpose: not only did it make Tom and Engel millionaires on paper, it enabled them to claim tax relief on all sort of things including the cost of concerts, staff, cars, and any other expenses concerned with their acts. The company meant more money for them and a greatly reduced tax bill.

If the idea for MAM and the title sounded rather sophisticated, there was a more simple meaning behind the name of the company. When Gordon and Tom talked about naming the company they got into a rather strange conversation about who they loved most, other than their wives. To the two men brought up in the valleys there was only one answer: 'My mam.' MAM was to stand as a tribute to both men's mothers and their deep love for them. Sentimentality and business are said not to mix, but in this case it worked. Gordon Mills was never one to stand still. Ideas were always formulating in his mind. Now he began to think that it was all very well having Tom and Engelbert living in England under his guidance, but they all lived miles away from each other: surely it would be better to keep his golden stable together in one area and exploit the superstar image even further?

In those days there were two kinds of pop stars. There were those that had a hit single and stayed forever in a small flat near the music industry's headquarters in London, maybe went a little further and bought themselves farms in Jersey or Ireland. But the real superstars did not muck about. During the 1960s the Beatles were the kings of the day, and where did John Lennon and George Harrison live? No less than St George's Hill, Weybridge, Surrey, a 250 acre money belt, green belt, shrine. It was considered the zenith of pop stardom habitats, the English equivalent of Beverly Hills, with rain. The locals had a nickname for it –'Heartbreak Hill', because if you reached the heights and income of St George's Hill, there was only one way to go and that was down. So called one-hit-wonders could not even dream of owning a house here. Lennon made it famous by travelling around the area in a psychedelic Rolls Royce. Cliff Richard was another inhabitant and lived at 'Feathergreen' with his friend Bill Latham and Bill's mother.

From a security and privacy point of view the place was perfect. Each home had its own magnificent drive shrouded by a plethora of green trees and hedges. To keep cranks away large dogs and security alarms were always in use. Nearby there is the St George's Hill Golf Club. Local shops catered for the absolute élite. The boutique had prices comparable with the high streets of Paris and the local motor car showroom sold Rolls-Royces which cost more than the average miner in South Wales earned in a lifetime. The food and wine shops were stocked to the hilt with the best pâtés, caviar, cheeses, fine wine and champagnes.

Each house was a complete and separate entity cordoned off by a red and white barrier, and for the pop stars there were closed circuit cameras in the trees and trip-switch spotlights to frighten off any crazy fan or intruder. Mills moved his pop family to Weybridge with the panache of a man who was recognized as being the biggest pop impresario in the world. Tom moved into a magnificent mansion, called 'Tor Point' which, by the early 70s, was valued at £400,000. Engelbert moved into a comparable mansion called 'Glenbrook' and Gordon himself, never forgetting his valley background, moved into 'Little Rhondda'. Tom, being the most famous of the three, had the most elaborate security precautions. The house was guarded by massive iron gates with Welsh griffins on the posts. For all three houses security men were also hired to give them the maximum amount of privacy. To keep himself fit, Tom later built himself a health complex complete with showers, sauna, and an L-shaped swimming pool with a dragon painted on the bottom.

The locals were honoured by it all, but these élite and famous neighbours had their strange ways. One woman wrote to a national newspaper saying she had spotted Tom at a local garage. She chatted to him and was surprised how friendly he was, considering he was supposed to be a superstar. After they had a natter Tom said goodbye but came back and asked for his Green Shield stamps. 'You don't save them, do you?' she asked. Pointing to his Rolls-Royce, Tom replied, 'How do you think I got this, then?'

If Tom asking for Green Shield stamps sounded a bit odd, Gordon was certainly one league ahead in appearing strange. He built a mini-zoo complete with tigers and gorillas. Gordon's favourite gorilla was called Ollie and was known to get up to all sorts of tricks. On one occasion Ollie ripped the dress off a female visitor and on another he attacked one of the zoo helpers. Gordon was so incensed on seeing this he punched it on the nose. Visitors to Gordon's house can recall seeing baby tigers lurking in the toilets, put there as a joke by Gordon. But it was not cruelty, he loved animals and would say outright that he preferred them to people anyway. His love for animals took him on regular safaris to Africa where he would take his old school chum Gordon 'Gog' Jones and band leader Johnny Spence who backed Tom on many of his big concerts. Gordon had created two medallion men and for the time being was happy with that. MAM diversified in the early 1970s and ventured into buying hotels, a yachting marina, and creating the largest hiring agency of amusement machines which included thousands of jukeboxes in pubs and clubs throughout Britain.

Under the auspices of MAM he began to take control of more than 100 artistes and one of his biggest successes in the early 1970s was Welsh rock singer Dave Edmunds. Edmunds hit the top of the charts in 1970 with 'I Hear You Knocking' and claimed that without Gordon he would never have done it. John Lennon was to call 'I Hear You Knocking' one of the best songs of the decade, and played it over and over again to friends. 'I Hear You Knocking' was the first single to be released on the MAM label. It was aptly catalogued as 'MAM ONE'. A former member of Tom's backing band — Micky Gee — played guitar on it. Gordon saw it as a good omen. After all, what other company could boast a number one hit with their first single?

But soon a third medallion man was to emerge, and from rather strange circumstances. A young Irish singer/songwriter called Raymond O'Sullivan wrote to Gordon enclosing tapes of himself and told him he had decided that Gordon was to be his manager. If it was blatant cheek, it worked. Gordon was caught by the young man's writing ability. O'Sullivan had also sent pictures of himself and it could be said that he was no great looker. But Gordon had a feeling about Raymond, who was the second son of six children born in Waterford. The O'Sullivans had moved to Swindon in Wiltshire and it was from there that Raymond was trying to make his name.

Gordon played Tom and Engel the tapes but they were none too impressed. The songs sounded fair enough, but the voice . . . well, it was different, far different from what they provided. Gordon arranged a meeting with Raymond O'Sullivan and afterwards told Tom, Engel, and stunned aides that this Irish hippy art student was going to be the next superstar. So taken aback were Tom and Engel that they forgot their own rivalry and merely stood back to watch the incredible scene. O'Sullivan arrived into the fold a shy retiring fellow with little or nothing to say. The other two found it hard to relate to him but they could sense that perhaps Gordon was right, there was something about the lad.

Gordon spent almost twelve months grooming his 'new superstar'. It was merely a matter of following the winning formula. Woodward had become Jones, Dorsey had become Humperdinck, and now

Raymond O'Sullivan was to change his name to Gilbert O'Sullivan — after two famous opera composers, W. S. Gilbert and Arthur Sullivan It had occurred to Gordon to complete the image by dressing O'Sullivan in a tuxedo like Jones and Humperdinck, but that was too predictable. O'Sullivan was younger than his other two singers. They appealed to a more mature market. Baby-faced Gilbert was to appeal to the teenyboppers, so his image had to be different. The first appearances of Gilbert O'Sullivan were treated with a great deal of mirth by the pop critics. They had never seen anything like him before. When O'Sullivan walked on stage he looked like the parody of an out of work 1930 miner. Flat cap, striped tie, oversize jacket, three-quarter length trousers, long socks and a pair of appalling lace-up work boots. The British public, however, if rather bemused, took to O'Sullivan like ducks to water. There was something about him, something different that made him stand out amongst the jungle of up-and-coming pop stars. When he climbed on to his piano on BBC's Top of the Pops it was a sheer joy to watch him, and his songs were extremely good, with a sentimental depth about them. Gordon tended to treat Gilbert as a boy. On nights out he would get him to babysit for his children and it was on one of these occasions O'Sullivan wrote the hit song 'Clair' after Gordon's daughter. Even after his first hit Gordon still only paid Gilbert pocket money of £IO per week, a fact that led to great amusement between Tom and Engelbert. But if they treated Gilbert with ironic disdain, the feeling was somewhat mutual.

O'Sullivan believed Tom and Engel were too old fashioned, appealing only to middle-aged housewives. Whereas he had a talent they did not possess — a talent for writing songs. In the early days of his success Gilbert tied in with his working class hero image. He had no Rolls-Royce, no big mansion and apart from babysitting he would sometimes make tea for people at the recording studios. He was a shy young man who preferred to travel by tube and initially shunned anything to do with the champagne high life of Weybridge.

For more than a year O'Sullivan kept up his absurd yet highly appealing cloth cap image. Some critics complained saying that the image was too silly and the joke was over. 'It's time for Gilbert O'Sullivan to come of age' the headlines screamed out. Gordon was quick to react. Within a few months, gone was the cloth cap and black boots, in came medallion man number three. Pictures of the time showed Gilbert with Afro hairdo, open neck shirt, hairy chest and the medallion shining mercilessly. On the back of such hits as 'Clair' and 'Alone Again, Naturally', Gilbert O'Sullivan had been canonized from being an unattractive boy into a sex symbol man. Gordon moved Gilbert from a flat in Notting Hill to a bungalow at St George's Hill. The new habitat was called 'Ebony House' and valued at £85,000. It was the smallest of the Mills clan houses. To tie in with the new macho image Gilbert was also supplied with a Mercedes. The problem was he could not drive, so he resorted to hiring his brother

Kevin to be his driver and road manager. Tom and Engel also noticed something else about Gilbert O'Sullivan: the remarkable similarities between him and Gordon. In the sex symbol photos he looked rather like a younger Gordon. And indeed Gordon in the early stages seemed to have affected

Gilbert to the extent that they had similar mannerisms. But perhaps it was a case of imitation being the greatest form of flattery, Gilbert was Gordon's 'baby' and like Tom and Engel, Gordon had made him great. Gordon's overwhelming personality had rubbed off on all of them but in Gilbert it was more noticeable. Gordon liked to keep firm control of his three medallion men. In some ways his relationship with Tom was rather like a marriage. Deep down they adored and respected each other but they would have their bust-ups. After one heated argument, Tom threatened to tear up his contract and suggested they both go their separate ways. The next day Tom called Gordon and they were friends again. Mills also had bust-ups with Engel. On one occasion he gave Engel 'a bollocking' for being late for a meeting, and when Engel said his car had broken down , Mills shouted even louder saying that he could have hired a taxi with all the money he was earning. It was said Engel was close to tears after feeling the wrath of Gordon's tongue. Engelbert felt a lot of bitterness at Gordon's attitude towards him. Throughout the years Engel was managed by Gordon he felt he was being treated as second best to Tom and was not getting the full and proper attention of his manager. Although the

Weybridge set-up was considered ideal for the Mills medallion men they barely had the chance to experience it. For up to eight months at a time Gordon, Engel and Tom would be away on tours, mostly in America — the US cabaret circuit provided their most lucrative work. For Linda it was to be a rather tedious period. For most of the time she stayed at home in Weybridge, and at one point she got so lonely she would dance alone to Tom's records into the early hours of the morning, imagining he was singing to her.

When Mark joined Tom on tour the situation was even worse. Linda would wait by the phone until the early hours of the morning to speak to her son and husband in America. Ninety per cent of the time they phoned her because she found it almost impossible to get through to Tom. If she tried to phone concert halls or hotels and said she was Tom's wife, the management would just yawn in disbelief; after all, they had heard that story a million times before and it was a standard ploy by fans attempting to get through to Tom.

For most of the time she stayed indoors. At times she resented the tag of being the wife of a sex-symbol superstar. After all, she was Linda Trenchard from little old Cliff Terrace, Treforest, not some glamorous model with a penchant for publicity. She felt that people were always looking at her and aware of her image. If someone rang the front door bell she wouldn't answer it unless she made-up her face and combed her hair. She was finding that being the wife of a superstar had its unusual pressures which impinged on everyday life — indoors or outdoors.

When Linda decided to visit Tom in America she found that she could not bear to see all those screaming women yearning for her man. She confined herself to the hotel room waiting for Tom to finish his act. Most of the time, even if he wanted to go out after the show to a party or just have a drink, Linda was content to stay in the hotel away from the showbiz razzmatazz circle.

From the early days she had been satisfied to keep in the background, away from the prying eyes and flashbulbs. She rarely went to any of Tom's shows and abhorred the idea of being pointed out in the audience as 'Tom Jones's wife' with people staring at her as though she was an exhibit in the zoo. Throughout it all she remained the typical valley wife, although she no longer lived there.

6. All Shook Up

The flower-power era had ended, and the 1970s brought in a kind of cynicism. The dreams of millions of hippies had come to nothing. Peace was what they wanted but still trouble raged throughout the world. The psychedelic music scene suddenly found itself all washed up. The hippy protesters outside the White House packed up, went home, got short haircuts and found themselves decent jobs. A lot of artistes were 'out' and hung their kaftans in the cupboard forever. But to Tom and Gordon it was a relief and they at least were still riding high. Tom had never felt settled with the crazy 1960s. He could not relate to the flower people because they were the complete opposites of what he believed in and what he had experienced in Pontypridd during the 1950s.He said, 'The way I see it, this is a man's world and you've got to fight to earn your feathers. I don't understand all these dropout kids. And I don't understand what any of them have got to protest about. My old man, until I made him give it up, was a miner. He worked down the pits all his life. When I see all these kids squatting down I feel like telling them where to get off and get some real work done for a change.' If Tom was disillusioned with the flower-power era and what it stood for, the feeling certainly seemed to be mutual.

A crazed flower-power maniac hippy called Charles Manson had big plans for Tom and they involved Tom not breathing again. Manson and his followers raided showbiz houses and slaughtered the inhabitants, stabbing and ripping them to pieces, before splattering their blood all over the walls. After murdering Roman Polanski's wife, Sharon Tate, they also murdered her unborn baby, writing word 'Pigs' on the walls in blood. Manson reckoned himself to be a good singer and guitarist. His theme tune was the Beatles' 'Helter Skelter' which he saw as a secret message warning him of a black uprising in America. Manson did not like Tom's singing, did not like him in any way because to him he represented the establishment and had to be wiped out. After some of the most brutal murders in American history Manson and his followers were arrested. The Los Angeles police told Tom they had found a murder list on Manson and his name was on it along with Frank Sinatra and Elizabeth Taylor.

Tom was only a whisker away from the plan being implemented. Manson had arranged for a very attractive girl to go to Tom's concert and sweet-talk her way backstage. A shaken Tom explained later, 'I was supposed to take her back to the hotel and while we were making love she was going to cut my throat with a razor.' No wonder Tom didn't like the flower-power people.

During the early 1970s the Jones fever was hotter than ever. He embarked on the biggest tour in American showbiz history, arranged by Buddy Howe, president of America's giant CMA agency, and the itinerary was even more ambitious than the Beatles' tours of 1964 and 1965 and the Rolling Stones' tour of the previous autumn. In April Tom starred for a month at the International Hotel, Las

Vegas. In May he appeared at New Jersey's Latin Hill Casino for two weeks.

Throughout June Tom was to play two nights at Madison Square Garden, New York, a fortnight at the Copacabana, and a series of one-nighters at the Los Angeles Forum, San Francisco's Cow Place, Dallas Memorial Auditorium, Houston Pavilion, Boston Gardens, Chicago Amphitheatre, Cincinnati Gardens, Cleveland Public Auditorium, Detroit Olympia Stadium, the Columbia Maryland and the Holmdel in New Jersey. In Canada he played the Toronto Maple Leaf Gardens and the Montreal Forum.

In July he was to play the Hampton Coliseum, Greenboro Auditorium in Nashville, Memphis Coliseum, Mobile Auditorium, Miami Convention Hall, Columbia Coliseum, Raleigh Coliseum, Charlotte Coliseum, Philadelphia Spectrum, Pittsburgh Civic Centre, Salt Lake City Palace, Phoenix Coliseum, and San Deigo Sports Centre. In all there were thirty-four one-night stands.

His shows were once again fully booked at the Copacabana in New York and at the International Hotel in Las Vegas — where Elvis had performed his comeback shows the year before. It was at the Copacabana in New York, Tom had problems with his voice which began to dry up after less than a week. Doing up to three shows a night at the club had taken its toll but he refused to cancel any of them. He decided to cut out the hard numbers like 'I Who Have Nothing', 'Without Love' and 'Venus' to give him a chance of carrying on. A specialist told him his throat was badly inflamed and ordered him to inhale steam from a basin of water. Gordon Mills could not cope with the offers coming in. Tom was to earn more than £2m from the tour. The media announced that he was the biggest crowd puller since the Beatles. And some said he was even above the heights of Frank Sinatra and Elvis because they had never played in front of such large audiences. At Madison Square he set a box office record of $364,743 gross. In Puerto Rico more than 28,000 screaming fans turned up at a sports stadium to pay homage to the singing Welshman, going bananas as Tom landed on stage by helicopter. The mayor was one of Tom's biggest fans and presented him with keys giving Tom the freedom of the city of San Juan. Gordon Mills said something which he was to say over and over again during his years of managing Tom. 'I don't think that Britain has realized how enormous Tom is in the States and the rest of the world. Britain still hasn't given him all the credit he deserves for becoming the world's number one superstar. He can't get any bigger than right now because he's right at the top. 'Success to Tom meant more money but less privacy. He was like a prisoner, confined to his hotel rooms. Even then privacy could be hard to find. Randy females out for what they could get would be up to all sorts of tricks.

Guards caught some posing as chambermaids, coming into the room to 'change the sheets on the beds'. Others called round with bowls of fruit saying they were with the manager's compliments. The more well-off hired uniforms and appeared at the door casually with fresh buckets of champagne which they had paid for out of their own pockets. Others, more careful with their money, just appeared with fresh ice for the buckets. One was even found by security guards in Tom's wardrobe waiting to pounce when he changed his clothes.

'Is there nothing these women won't do to try and get to Tom?' an exasperated hotel manager was heard to say. At the New York Hilton Tom was paying four hundred pounds a day for his suite but considered it more of a jail. He had to take to wearing a false beard to go for a walk in nearby Central Park with one of his bodyguards. Shopping was also difficult. He followed Elvis's example and had department stores open just for him after hours. Perhaps the stress of doing so many gigs got to Tom at times. He was singing at a place called Pine Knob in America when to an astounded audience he appeared to lose his temper and began to kick flowers, which fans had thrown at his feet, all over the stage. But worst of all he was seen to spit at the pianist. After the show Tom dismissed it all as a joke. He said everything had gone wrong that night — the PA system had blown up, the lighting was faulty — and he had kicked the flowers away because he did not want to slip on the highly polished floor as they were like banana skins. He said spitting at the pianist was part of the joke and it was all in good fun.

The Copacabana tended to be a repeat of previous years. As thousands of females clamoured for him to come on stage Tom was frightened that he would be scratched to death by their long fingernails. He had to be carried to the stage by three well-built guards through an avenue of waiters. Newspapers described it as being performed as a military operation. Mills did not want his man injured, especially when any injury could set them back a million dollars in gigs.

Tom was becoming a very expensive item. He was advised to keep a towel on his head to stop fans pulling his hair out as he went on stage. When leaving the Club a police escort waited, sirens screaming, to take him away. Things got so out of control that even the Duke of Windsor, who was staying at the Waldorf Astoria, said he was amazed at the security precautions for this man Jones. As the ex-king of England he had never been offered anything like that sort of protection.

In his first week at the Las Vegas International Hotel his bookings were reckoned to be double that of his rivals in the town. His rivals? Oh, just Frank Sinatra, Johnny Carson and Dean Martin. In a month of shows Tom grossed $550,000.

While at the International Tom met up with Elvis Presley again. Elvis's confidence had taken a boost now that he was back on the live circuit and he once again thanked Tom for giving him the inspiration to do it. Indeed the previous year, when Elvis had made his come-back at the International, critics and fans alike noticed how much Elvis had copied from Tom's stage act. What Elvis had learned from Tom was the trick of working a Las Vegas show. Tom made Elvis realize that you had to be over the top, dynamic, and highly sexual, and get through to the middle-aged females who made up the majority of the audiences.

To a great extent, for his Vegas act, Elvis copied Tom's headshaking, poses and phrasing in songs. He also picked up the trick of wiping his sweaty brow with a cloth and tossing it to the frenzied audience. But he did not want to rip-off Tom completely, he had to appear different. He would not wear a tuxedo and 'spray-on' tight trousers. He would wear something which he considered to be more potently sexual, powerful, and physically dynamic: a karate suit, a 'gi'.

Elvis was fanatical about karate and was a black belt. He transformed what he learned from Tom's act into karate movements and his moves during the show were seen as brilliant choreography to go with the songs. Tom had the tuxedo, Elvis had the gi in black mohair. He pranced about the stage throwing karate kicks and punches, showing his skill not only as a singer but as a fighter as well. Some critics saw it as a childish fascination with violence but the audiences loved it right to the very last song, karate chop and kick.

At one after-show party Tom and Elvis met again. Before, Tom had been in awe of the legend and Elvis had talked to Tom like a father, but this time they spoke to each other on a firm ground as familiar friends. If anything Elvis appeared to take the 'big brother' attitude because of his vast musical and acting experience in America. That particular night they got on brilliantly and then Elvis started talking about his act and his love — karate. Tom teased Elvis, saying that karate was just like street fighting and boxing was a far more noble and sophisticated form of self-defence. In good humour Elvis took this as a sort of challenge and they began showing each other various moves in their respective sports.

The moves became rather boisterous and anyone coming into the room would have thought that Tom and Elvis were having a fight, but to both of them it was a way of having fun and showing their friendship for each other. After this rather unusual demonstration of boxing and karate the two superstars could not stop laughing. Priscilla Presley was right — every time Tom and Elvis got together they were like two schoolboys.

Tom might have been singing at the International Hotel but he had to give up living there because of constant female intruders in the wee small hours. At times there was also trouble with angry husbands demanding their room keys back after their wives had thrown them on stage. They were told all room keys were returned to reception. Tom decided to move to a 'safe house' a few miles away to get some peace. He even had to give up using his white Lincoln Continental limousine because his fans were ambushing it every time it hit the road. For security reasons and more privacy Tom rode in inconspicuous cars and trucks to get to and from shows.

It was the same all over the country. At one point Tom would say, 'Bloody hell, even Cassius Clay would have trouble fighting this lot.'

At a show in New Jersey who should walk in? Cassius Clay, otherwise known as Muhammad Ali. Tom was performing at the Latin Casino, Cherry Hills, New Jersey, when Muhammad Ali came in after the show with his daughter and soon put his famous mouth into action. 'I'm just her father but you're her superstar.' Muhammad told Tom that he had watched all his shows on TV and the first words his daughter had uttered were 'Tom Jones'!

Muhammad said he thought Tom was 'the greatest' in showbiz. To pardon the pun, Tom was knocked-out and arranged for all of his albums to be sent to Ali's daughter. In return Ali sent him a pair of his boxing gloves. Afterwards Tom went to see Ali whenever possible.

Tom was to meet another personality who took his breath away — Jane Fonda. Tom appeared with her on TV in New York and much to his surprise he found the actress shaking with nerves and highly agitated. Tom asked her why, she replied, 'It's easy for you. You are you all the time. When I go in front of the public I have to think of my image.' Tom commented, 'I hadn't thought of it like that before, but it's quite true. I don't change when I am on stage.'

After the exhausting tour Tom decided to go on holiday in August and where better than the sunny climate of Mexico? Eat, drink and be merry. That's what he thought, anyway. The local alcohol was certainly different, but it was the hot spicy food that was to have a lingering effect. He flew back to Los Angeles to record eight shows for the This Is Tom Jones TV series, but found Mexico had caught up with him. A violent pain raged through his stomach and he became feverish. Tom thought he was near to death and at one point it got pretty serious. He said, 'It was terrible. I couldn't eat and they fed me through a vein in my wrist. Then as quickly as the pains came, they went, thank God.'

After recording the shows over two months Tom arrived back in Britain in October and although it was supposed to be hush-hush more than thirty fans were waiting for him at the airport. It took him two hours to get through customs and they charged him £275 duty on the presents he had brought back home. He had to borrow the money to pay. Good old Britain. Back down to earth with a bump! By the early 1970s Tom had firmly made his mark throughout the world. He had successes in countries where no other English speaking singer had. In Israel some reckoned his records were selling faster than kosher food. He was consistently top of the Israeli charts and had been voted the most popular foreign singer with the now legendary 'Delilah'. The Jews and Arabs might have had their own kind of music but when it came to singing the Welshman was considered tops. It was the same story in Spain where 'Delilah' stayed for more than fifteen weeks at the top of the charts. Tom's appearances in the late sixties in Barcelona, Madrid, and Palma, Majorca, resulted in boosting sales into their hundreds of thousands. 'I'm Coming Home' stayed top for three weeks and 'Help Yourself' was in the top five for eleven weeks. In some areas Tom was more popular than bullfights and he was consistently voted best foreign singer in all the Spanish polls. 'Delilah' alone amounted to more than 150,000 Spanish sales. When it comes to singing, language is no barrier and in Norway and Sweden the reaction was the same. In Norway there was no one to rival Tom when it came to appealing to the middle-aged females and sales rocketed. In Sweden 'The Green, Green Grass of Home' and 'Love Me Tonight' contributed to sales of 150,000 singles. Tom had played Sweden in 1967 with the Squires but it was the This Is Tom Jones series, shown on the Swedish Broadcasting Corporation, which led to the success of the singles and by 1970 the sales of 240,000 albums. Some of the Swedish stars reckoned they were witnessing a goldmine in action and covered some of Tom's songs and they themselves sold records in their thousands. In Denmark, Holland, Finland, Belgium, France, Switzerland, Germany, and even the communist countries Yugoslavia and Bulgaria, the Jones fever was evident. In the communist countries Tom was so popular his records were produced under licence. In Czechoslovakia, Tom's records were also covered by other artistes and an order for 22,000 copies of his albums was placed by the Czechoslovakian Record Club.

In so-called staid Germany, 'Delilah' earned Tom a gold record with more than 1,000,000 sales. In France, after making a few appearances in Paris, the fever spread, leading to equally vast sales. In Finland he followed in the steps of Elvis Presley and was voted best singer. In Belgium he was the most played pop singer on radio. In Switzerland every release made it into the top twenty. In Holland Tom had made no personal appearances and was featured only briefly on his imported TV show, but he still managed to get a gold record selling around 100,000 copies of 'Delilah'. By 1971 Gordon Mills was proud to boast that Tom had sold more than 100 million records worldwide, and there were more to come!

But Tom had enemies in the showbiz world who started malicious rumours about other women in his life. The British singer Kathy Kirby was the subject of one of these lies. A rumour had gone round that she had had Tom's baby. Kathy and Tom both laughed off the absurd rumour but she found to her horror that people were believing it and even becoming venomous about it. A letter was delivered with her fan mail to the Midlands hotel she was staying in. It said, 'Kathy Kirby. When giving your next interview I suggest you discuss the merits of stealing other people's husbands and producing your little bastards. People who live in the Midlands, who have heard of your latest additions, feel sickened to see you smiling away so smugly and innocent. So next time you think of hiding away to have your illegitimate children remember there will always be someone to spread the news.' It may have come from one of Tom's fanatical and jealous fans who tended to react violently if they heard any rumours of him with another woman. At another show a man shouted from the audience, 'How's Tom Jones's bastard?' while Kathy was singing. It became too much and she broke down on stage and rushed off in tears. When she came back on the stage she apologized to the audience, saying that one poor sick mind could not stop her.

To those who knew Kathy and Tom the suggestion of them having an affair and an illegitimate child was highly ludicrous. Tom had been on a brief tour with her during the late 1960s, and that was as far as it went. The relationship was purely professional.

Tom thought it was a huge joke and said to Kathy, 'Did you hear that we're supposed to have had a baby together Kathy?' Kathy Kirby, although the victim of a cruel lie still managed to keep her sense of humour saying, 'You should be so lucky.' 'It should be a beautiful baby,' Tom said. 'Not if it looks like you!' replied Kathy.

The laughs were there amid the heartache, but to this day Kathy Kirby maintains that the lie was spread by show business rivals plotting to destroy her career. In the early 1970s life for Tom Jones must have seemed like one big tour whether that was in Britain, Europe, or the USA, but he still managed to find time to relax with Linda and Mark in Weybridge.

Tom had always been a great film fan and turned the top floor of his home into a private cinema. A snooker table was also in evidence and Tom would invite neighbours such as Matt Monroe and a great pal from the old days — comedian Jimmy Tarbuck — over to play. If he tired of the private cinema or snooker, he always had his swimming pool and squash court. At times he would head down to a nearby pub where the regulars treated him just like any other local. Or he could always have a drink in his own personal lounge bar at the house. Jimmy Tarbuck would join him for a drink and try to get him to play golf. Tarbuck is a self-confessed golf fanatic and has said he could play it all day. He called for Tom one morning early but Tom was still in bed and would not get up for anything. Tarbuck joked, 'You're nothing but a ruddy vampire. You only go to bed when the sun goes up.'

If there is one thing Tom likes, it is a good sleep and a long one at that. If anyone criticized this practice he would say, 'The longer you sleep, the more you can rest your vocal chords.' With vocal chords worth millions of dollars who could blame him? But perhaps sleep performed another function — a release from the extreme pressures of worldwide fame. Tom explained in one interview, 'I don't know anyone who can sleep during the day like me. If they didn't wake me up at 5 p.m. I could sleep until six.'

Apart from his friends in the Mills showbiz fraternity — Engelbert, Gordon, and Johnny Spence — Tom was never short of company. There was Linda and Mark, and then he brought his sister Sheila and her husband Ken Davies to Weybridge. He employed his brother-in-law as a general handyman—gardener. Sheila and Ken lived in a small lodge in the grounds of Tom's house.

He did not stop there; he also arranged for his mother and father to move from Sunbury to Weybridge to complete the family unit. Tom and his dad would go down to the local and knock back a few jars just like they would if they had stayed in the valleys. His proud father would often recall to regulars at the local, 'Tom always thought he was going to be a miner like his dad. When he was little he used to walk about in my pit boots with the steel tips and sometimes he'd put on my bowler as well. He did look comical.'

Tom's equally proud mother, Freda, boasted not of Tom's generosity after he became a star but of when he was a child. She would show neighbours and friends a little black elephant, which was four inches long and had cost Tom thirteen bob when he was a schoolboy. Tom, then aged ten, had been to Bristol Zoo on a school outing and blown all his savings on the little elephant. Freda recalled scolding him for spending all his money. But Tom replied, 'You're worth it, mam.'

If anything, that summed up how Tom Jones felt towards his parents. Even after he made it big his first concern was seeing that they were all right. Apart from Linda, they were the great love of his life. He adored them and would become upset if anything appeared wrong with them. When Tom was made a lucrative offer to take his clothes off and show all for a nude centrefold in Cosmopolitan he refused.

People thought it was strange that a so-called sex symbol was refusing to take his clothes off but Tom was straight to the point: 'My mother wouldn't like it.' Sometimes he became concerned about his father's health. His dad, after all the years down the pits, had trouble breathing at times. It upset Tom, but for all his wealth there was nothing he could do to change the past or his father's ways — Tom Snr, like all miners, liked a cigarette, even with his bad chest, and it worried Tom.

Gordon Mills was happy with what he had achieved. MAM had become highly profitable, Tom, Gilbert, and Engel were all world famous and he believed he had everything worked out to a fine art.

There was only one thing that annoyed him — living in Britain. As far as he was concerned Tom did not get the same recognition in Britain and Europe as he did in America where, like Presley, he was treated as some kind of living legend. The money and offers were bigger in America so, using the experience and model of the 1970 tour, Tom's main source of work was to be in the USA.

Phenomenal offers were coming in from Vegas, where the big money was. By comparison Britain could only offer what was considered by Gordon to be 'peanuts'. So it came to be that Tom did 90 per cent of his work in the USA and became a firm mainstay in the gambling capital of the world.

Tom was treated like royalty there. In the presidential suite at Caesar's Palace he was surrounded by an abundance of food and Dom Perignon champagne. He said in the early 70s, 'Las Vegas is the next best thing to home for me. The only trouble is it's like working down the mines in Wales — I seldom see the daylight!' Each night after the show to around 2,000 people Tom would stay up until the early hours of the morning and then sleep until 1 p.m. To keep his weight down, he would work out in the hotel's health club.

He would also subject himself to steam treatment on his vocal chords. In Las Vegas the dry desert air tends to get to the best of singers and it is not unknown for shows to be cancelled because throats have dried up. Famous singers like Tom avoid the open air and some remain virtual prisoners in their air-conditioned rooms until their show begins. Tom rationed himself to a brief time outside at 6.30 p.m. for some late sunbathing. Before the show at 8.30 p.m. he would have a small steak and a glass of orange juice.

Las Vegas itself is an artificial and incongruous city stuck in the middle of a desert. Inside the hotels and casinos it is the land of eternal light, the gambling action goes on twenty-four hours a day and clocks are noticeable by their absence. The clients vary from tourists who have saved for a blowout on the slot machines hoping that they'll be able to win a million dollars in one go, to the more sophisticated players who spend their time at the gambling tables until their last dollar drops. At times many of the punters look like glassy-eyed robots programmed to feed dollars into the hungry one-armed bandits.

On the other hand, in the early 1970s you had the Arabs. They were loaded with oil money and wanting to spend, spend, spend, with no thought or remorse about losing. One Arab father and his son wanted to bet millions of dollars at one casino. But the management were frightened they might win and wipe them out, so the casino put a limit of $100,000 dollars gambling money on each of them per night.

Some go away rich but the majority go away poorer. Down to their last dime and gallon of petrol they leave this artificial gambling kingdom and vow never to return again. But they always do the following year, armed with savings and a new optimism about their luck. In between this money mania Tom Jones performed to about 2,000 people nightly. The rich fans come and gamble and sleep in the best hotels. The poorer ones abstain from gambling and sleep in cars just to see their hero.

For Tom, Vegas was the chance to mix with the right crowd. He continued his friendship with Elvis Presley and when they were both appearing in Las Vegas at the same time there would be a friendly rivalry. Huge placards would proclaim 'Elvis Presley is at the International' and for pure cheek Tom's publicists put up other placards saying 'Tom Jones is in town.' Such was the relationship between the two men that when Tom was doing his act on stage Elvis would walk on unannounced and they would have a friendly banter in front of the startled audience. Fans expecting Elvis and Tom to sing in duet were disappointed. It never happened. Elvis had been warned by his manager Col. Tom Parker of the danger of hidden microphones and recordings which could impinge upon standing agreements with his record company.

A record of Tom and Elvis singing together would have been worth millions, even as a bootleg, but although it never happened on stage it did happen many times behind the stage at parties when they would sing rock and roll numbers all night and would even include the odd gospel song. Unfortunately nobody bothered to record these harmonic gatherings. On one occasion Tom and his father went to see Elvis's show. Afterwards Elvis sent for Tom and invited him back to his dressing room. Tom went in and told Elvis he was with his father. Elvis said, 'That's fine, bring him in. I've got my father with me too.' Tom Snr said after meeting Elvis and his father Vernon, 'Elvis is a nice fella and he thinks a lot of Tom.'

Tom Snr was right, Elvis did think a lot of Tom and their friendship was to grow during their days in Las Vegas. The two superstars would pass the whole night swapping stories of their childhood and discussing the meaning of life. A lot of the time the conversation centred on what had made both of them famous — music.

Elvis told Tom he didn't have much patience with 'the modern stuff'. In his mind he didn't think anything had happened musically since the 1950s. Tom agreed. Elvis confessed to Tom that he didn't even have copies of his old Sun records because he 'hated the rotten sound' and the only thing he liked about his later records was the cleaner sound and production. During one conversation Tom said to Elvis that it was a shame the Beatles had decided to break up. Elvis came to the conclusion that they couldn't handle the success and he asked Tom how he managed it. Tom said he would relax by having a cigar and a little champagne. He advised Elvis, 'Relax, take it easy, have fun with it. Enjoy it.'

Elvis said he had tried everything to relax. But at that time Tom was not aware that Elvis was becoming hooked on drugs. Tom noticed though that Elvis's aides tended to keep him away from reality. They constantly shielded him from ordinary people and a normal environment. 'Maybe part of the trouble was that he was held away from the public too much by the people who managed him,' Tom recalled.

Elvis told Tom his weight had continued to cause him problems. Tom said he had some problems with his own weight and advised Elvis to watch it daily by checking the bathroom scales. Tom said, 'He would always get his weight down when he had to. But towards the end it looked like nobody had any control over him. He just got bigger and bigger. I'd been seeing Elvis since 1965 and every time I saw him he was never the same weight. He would either be thin or heavy. He only seemed a normal weight once, around 1969 to 1970.'

Elvis' weight did seem to be a problem. He had a strange diet. His favourite food was hamburgers and it was nothing for him to consume dozens of them during the course of a day. He also tended to drink large quantities of Coca-Cola. Eating and drinking like this did nothing to improve his waistline and sometimes it was an effort to get into tight fitting clothes. Tom would recall later how he had seen an aide follow Elvis into the toilet and then help untie

The King's lace-up leather trousers. When Elvis was finished the aide then tied up the fly again because the trousers were so tight.

Elvis gave Tom a book on religious teachings saying, 'It really has been a great source of inspiration to me.' The two superstars then began to exchange gifts. Elvis gave Tom a chain bearing the initials TCB (Take Care of Business) and on another occasion he handed Tom a beautiful black sapphire ring. In return Tom bought Elvis a very expensive tiger's eye ring.

Elvis' generosity was not confined to gifts; when Tom landed himself in a spot of bother with his backing group, Elvis stepped in to help. Tom had come on stage in Vegas and made a joke about the Ku Klux Klan to which his black backing singers took exception. They refused to do any more shows. Elvis heard about

Tom's trouble and was on the phone straight away to New York. He had a new group of backing singers flown in from the Big Apple, but when they arrived Gordon and Tom had sorted out the trouble and the show went on as usual. Instead of sending the replacement singers back to New York, Elvis kept them on for a week and every night at after-show get togethers they entertained both Tom and Elvis. At times when Tom and Elvis would talk they would come up with ideas that seemed beyond anyone's imagination. Elvis once said to him, 'You know what we should do, Tom? We should do a show together but this show will be different. You'll stand at one end of the stage and I'll stand at the other end and we'll have the Beatles standing in the middle backing us.' Needless to say, it never became a reality The Beatles had met Elvis once during their first tour of America. A meeting was set up between the group and Elvis by their respective managers, Brian Epstein and Col. Tom Parker. Elvis agreed on the condition that the Beatles go to him and not he to them. The Beatles turned up at a house he had rented, between filming, at Perugia Way, Los Angeles, and had a jam with The King. But a few years later in an interview John Lennon confessed he had not been too impressed. He said, 'It was very disappointing. It was like meeting Engelbert Humperdinck.'

Although Tom and Elvis would stay up all night enthusing about American showbiz life, it also had a dark side to it. After receiving a couple of death threats Elvis was going through a paranoid phase and was convinced a crazy fan could kill him. He took to carrying a gun. He thought Tom was in the same position and sent along an aide to Tom's dressing room and told him to give him a gun as a present. Tom thanked Elvis for the rather unusual gift but thankfully he never had a need to use it.

7. Impossible Dream

If Elvis had his 'Memphis Mafia' with Sonny West and the boys, then Tom had his own comparable 'Valley Mafia'. There was Chris Ellis, from Nantgarw, near Pontypridd, Gordon 'Gog' Jones _ Gordon Mills' old school friend and fellow ex-bus conductor from Tonypandy — Rocky Seddon, a former boxer from Liverpool, and later Dai Perry, an old schoolmate of Tom's from Treforest. Dark haired, six feet tall, Dai was fiercely loyal to Tom. If you talked to the man he seemed quiet enough but if anyone made a move to harm Tom he could be a heavy piece of machinery, and like a bulldog would not let go until his master was out of danger.

Like Tom, Dai had been brought up the hard way on the streets of Treforest and had fought many a battle. His loyalty to Tom was something beyond mere money, it was a loyalty that stretched back to their childhood. A strong bond existed between them and they had a deep brotherly affection for each other. At gigs when screaming fans tried to tear Tom's clothing off or pull his hair out for a souvenir, it was always Dai to the rescue. Quick and straight to the point, no messing about. He brushed aside the more violent fans like flies and his muscular body surrounded Tom like an impregnable force. Dai was a solid Welshman and a handy guy to have around. He not only proved himself at concerts. In Wisconsin an intruder tried to gate-crash a party for Tom. He was asked to leave and when he became abusive Dai knocked him out. At Madison Square Garden Tom came off stage and was instantly overpowered by fans. His shirt was gone, so was the chain round his neck, and his trousers were ripped to shreds. The only reason Tom himself did not get hurt was because big Dai had managed to fend them off. The police in all their numbers could not handle it but Dai like the bulldog had got his master out in one piece.

Tom had been hitting the headlines for eight years but on 16 October 1973 he and Dai were to hit the headlines for other than musical reasons. On the way to Kennedy Airport in New York, Tom had a blazing row with Linda. They had been in a bad mood with each other all day. As the limousine headed towards the airport Linda shouted to Tom that sometimes she wished he had never made it and then they could have lived a normal life like everyone else in Treforest. Tom made a remark about the expense of his wife's jewellery and she promptly threw most of it out of the car window. At the airport Tom and his entourage, including Dai Perry, had a 'going home' celebration before boarding the flight. On the Jumbo the champagne continued to flow for the Jones party in the first class lounge. The party became a bit loud and boisterous. During the in-flight movie a woman objected to the noise. Tom had put his headphones on and was listening to a music programme. As Tom spoke to the rest of his party and tapped his fingers to the music the woman told him to keep quiet. Tom told her in rather rude terms to go away and she threw a cup of coffee over him. Tom threw a brandy back at the woman. A man in a uniform appeared to be approaching Tom so Dai leaped upon him pinning him to the ground. As other cabin staff approached, Dai warned them that they would get the same treatment if they tried anything. Dai shouted, 'You're not getting up until the plane lands' to which the man replied, 'The plane can't land without me, I'm the captain. 'Dai let him up and allowed him to return to his cabin. The captain radioed for help and asked for police to meet the plane at Heathrow Airport. When the plane landed, the heat of the moment had died down and a hush-hush approach was taken by the airline officials. Nothing more was said or done about the incident. But the Jones party had to wait for two hours while their bags were checked through customs. They had to pay a total of £850 excess duty before they were allowed to leave.

As they left the customs Tom and Dai were snapped by press photographers in a rather 'playfully aggressive mood'. The photos show Tom with a glazed look in his eyes and a clenched fist, looking at the equally glazed Dai who also had a clenched fist and a large grin on his face.

Perhaps during the preceding hours they had both relived the spirit of their Teddy boy days in Pontypridd. Both looked wild and happy in the photographs which were splashed all over the front pages of the tabloid newspapers in Britain.
A Pan-Am spokesman said, 'This whole affair is most regrettable. We have been carrying Mr Jones and his party on most of his round-the-world tour and this is the first time anyone has complained about them.'

Tom said at the airport, 'Sure there was a party. After all, we have been away for six months. We celebrated — wouldn't you?'

A few minutes later Dai was earning his money and friendship again as he and a rather frightened looking policeman kept Tom away from the sharp claws of thirty shrieking fans. Towards the end of 1973 Tom came into contact with one of the world's most beautiful women, nineteen-year-old Marjorie Wallace who had just been voted Miss World.

If anything Marji Wallace had begun her career rather more flamboyantly than previous winners of the title. Past winners of this accolade had been all smiles with hidden private lives, but to the newspapers Marji Wallace was good material — she appeared to be a bit of a flirt. Her boyfriend racing driver Peter Reveson was in America, but she managed to appear happy without him, and she hit the front pages in November 1973 by kissing Tom's fellow medallion man Engelbert Humperdinck at the Miss World Ball.

It was rumoured that Engel quite fancied this tall leggy American lady but it all came to nothing. A month later in December she went backstage to meet Tom at the London Palladium. Tom admired her stunning looks and joked when they met, 'Do I have to go down on my knees for you?' Marji was amused by the Jones cheek. She was quick with a put down, 'I thought you already were.'

People who witnessed the meeting reckoned something had clicked between them. The gossip columnists had a field day saying there certainly seemed to be something going on between the world's top singing sex symbol and Miss World. What a story! And how it would sell papers! Julia and Eric Morley, who controlled both Mecca's Miss World competition and Marji's career, were not pleased with this flirtish image and tried to tone down any suggestions that their Miss World was a good-time girl. If Tom and Marji had met socially they were also to meet again professionally when they were signed up to do a BBC TV spectacular in Barbados in 1974, Tom Jones on Happiness Island. The idea was that Tom Jones as a superstar would meet super girl Miss World on an idyllic romantic location. In one scene Marji was to stroll hand in hand with Tom along the beach and then they were to get into a romantic embrace, kissing passionately. During filming Julia Morley was furious and ordered Marji not to kiss Tom because it would create the wrong sort of image for the 'pure' Miss World. Marji showed contempt for Julia Morley's suggestion and the proposed kiss took place for all the world to see. Mrs Morley was famous for her strictness and temper with Miss World girls, and Marji had crossed her. This was reckoned to be a fatal thing to do. The kiss had, as Julia Morley predicted, fuelled rumours of a romance between Tom and Marji. Speculation rose even further when they were seen together at various bars on the island and at Tom's house.

If that scenario was not explosive enough, Marji certainly did her best to make it more explosive. After flying back to England, she got herself involved with soccer legend George Best. She met him at a nightclub while Tom was in Holland and both of them were pictured leaving the place. Best, although a genius at his game, had had a turbulent career. His days at Manchester United had made him a soccer superstar but his heavy drinking sessions, habit of not turning up for training, and his continual womanizing tagged him with a bad boy glamour image which would ultimately end his career. Marji was seen on the town with the handsome Irishman, and to the newspapers things could not be better. She was now connected with Best, Jones and Reveson, all sex symbols in their own right.

Best and Wallace were rumoured to be having a steamy relationship and Best was said to be jealous of Tom Jones. The rumours heightened when Marji finished off filming the TV special with Tom in London. After the show was completed Marji was often seen in Tom's company and this angered the Morleys even further. The final straw was when Marji called the police to her hotel and accused George Best of stealing her fur coat and some jewellery. The gossip columnists went to town, claiming that Marji's love diary had also gone missing.

The diary was supposed to have had marks out of ten for the men she had been with. Journalists out for a hot story put the speculation to Marji that she had given Tom nine out of ten and Best a lowly three. Marji said it was malicious gossip and a fantastic rumour. Best denied the theft and told police that he and Marji had been close lovers. Marjorie denied the intimate details, saying Best had pestered her.

In the event, the Morleys thought enough was enough, and Marji was stripped of her Miss World crown after only 104 days. Best was later cleared in a sensational court case where he said he and Marji had made love in her hotel room and then she had phoned her unknowing boyfriend Peter Reveson while Best was still in the bedroom.

Two weeks after she was stripped of her title, Reveson was killed in a car crash in South Africa.

When Tom played Vegas that year Marji was also in town but both still denied any rumours of romance. Marji was staying at Peter Reveson's sister's house in Los Angeles, and she told Jennifer Reveson that Tom was 'a friend and nothing more'. She admitted to Jennifer that she had 'led Tom on a bit in Britain and Barbados' but nothing had happened between them physically. Reveson's sister joined Marji when she went to meet Tom and Gordon Mills for lunch at a restaurant in Beverly Hills. They were not Jennifer Reveson's type — she found them boring. During the lunch Tom talked about his career and Gordon about the money the stars and he had made. Jennifer could see that Tom appeared very friendly towards Marji and felt angry that her dead brother seemed to have been forgotten as a thing of the past.

When she relayed her feelings, Marji was said to have replied, 'Why shouldn't I go out with Tom if he wants me to? I just don't care what people think. I like Tom and he likes me. That's all that matters.' Marji flew off to Las Vegas and was seen with Tom again but both maintained they were just friends, although one restaurant manager said they seemed very affectionate towards each other.

Tom may have enjoyed his friendship with Marji Wallace but all the publicity meant that his marriage to Linda was suffering. Gordon warned him that the publicity with Marji could spell big trouble and he was advised to end his friendship with the beautiful former Miss World. Soon afterwards Marji, back in her home town of Indianapolis, took an overdose of drugs and was rushed to hospital in a coma. Newspapers reported that she had taken at least four bottles of sleeping pills. Certainly, for several crucial days Marji was on the critical list and near to dying. At first the news was kept from Tom. The media speculated that her overdose was to do with her friendship with him.

When Marji came off the critical list her father Del Wallace said, 'She told me Mr Jones had been a good friend to her. And God knows a girl who has been through Marji's ordeal needs a friend.' A press release was given out saying, 'Tom is very happy that Marji is getting better and feels that things are being said about her character when she is not in the position to defend herself.' Throughout the crucial week Tom's camp and Marji's relatives insisted that there had been no romance between them. He sent Marji a get-well telegram. At the same time he was pictured blowing out the candles at his 34th birthday party at Caesar's Palace with his Las Vegas showbiz friends including Liberace, Joan Rivers, Sonny Bono, Dionne Warwick and Debbie Reynolds.

During 1974 the Tom Jones roadshow was a major feature of the world's concert circuit. Gordon believed he had laid the foundations of success and it was merely a matter of building on these foundations by simply repeating the process. Another world tour was organized and Tom was to visit Japan and the volatile South America. Tom had visited Japan on an earlier occasion and thousands turned out to see him. At each Japanese town he stopped the traffic. South America was a different kettle of fish. Engelbert Humperdinck had been in Venezuela some time earlier and when going through customs was held for having a bottle of pills in his baggage. When asked about them, Engel replied that they were to calm his nerves and to help his voice. He was held for more than an hour while tests were run on the pills, which were found to be tranquillizers and vitamin pills. Engel was shocked at how rude and abusive the Venezuelan customs men had been and vowed he would never return.

Throughout the tour there had been rumours of a plot to kidnap Mark and all the Jones entourage were extremely nervous. When they arrived in Caracas, Venezuela, the nervousness showed through as a sea of dark-skinned faces clamoured to see Tom when he walked through the airport. The screaming and shouting from the hordes did not make things any better. Caracas certainly seemed to be a crazy place full of crazy people and there could be one out there in the crowd with a gun waiting to end it all.

As Tom fought his way to get through the crowds Dai Perry did his best to protect him. As tensions rose Dai, fed up with being pushed and jostled by the crowd, turned round and punched a man on the face. The loud crack from Dai's fist resounded through the crowd and on the floor lay photographer Manola Olaquiaga. He told the police that Dai had hit him for no reason and wanted to press charges. Dai maintained that the photographer had struck him first but it seemed the police were on the Venezuelan's side.

When Tom and the entourage reached the Hilton Hotel they learned that the photographer planned to take Dai to court and was demanding a detention order be served on him the next day. Gordon Mills had been none too pleased about the Jumbo bust up the year before and it was decided that Dai had to go for the sake of himself and the rest of the party. He flew out on an early morning flight before the photographer could obtain the order to arrest him. Two days later the tension was still there but the Jones entourage had concluded that now Dai was out of the way the Venezuelans would take no further action. They were wrong. When they arrived at the airport after an all-night champagne drinking session the customs man checking their passports shook his head and said, 'You cannot leave.'

The shocked party, now virtually imprisoned in Caracas, asked the British Embassy to help, but help was slow in forthcoming. Ensconced in their hotel suite they called in lawyers but were told the case could drag on for months. To ease the tension a bit of light relief came in the form of Tom having his photograph taken with handcuffs on and two smiling guards prodding guns into his body. The pictures were later splashed all over the world.

But the reality of the situation was no laughing matter. It was decided to send a cable to the then Prime Minister, Harold Wilson, asking him for his immediate help. The cable read, 'Implore the assistance of Her Majesty's Government in securing release of British citizen Tom Jones who has been refused permission to leave Venezuela because of an incident in which he was not personally involved. ' The words sounded grand enough but they meant little. The British Government had their hands tied in a volatile country like Venezuela.

Harold Wilson instructed British officials to do what they could but in such countries there is only one way to get out of trouble and that is when money speaks rather loudly. A man claiming to be a lawyer phoned the hotel suite and told the Jones entourage that he had set up a meeting with one of Venezuela's high ranking judges who, it was learned, had given the photographer a detention order against them. The man said the Judge would meet Tom before 8 a.m. and he was to bring a substantial amount of money — $12,000.

In countries such as Venezuela Gordon insisted that they be paid in cash so they had enough money in the hotel suite to take to the court. When they arrived the next morning the judge met Tom in a room and he was told to leave the money in a briefcase with a man in the next office. A private deal had been worked out. The judge told Tom a plane was leaving the country within an hour and he'd better be on it. He said that if Tom was not on the plane the court would be re-opened and he would have no choice but to extend the photographer's detention order. A mad dash was made to the airport and Tom gave a great sigh of relief as the plane left the tarmac leaving Caracas well and truly behind. Tom said, 'It was like a bad dream. Until they took the aircraft steps away and closed the door I was half expecting someone to grab me by the arm and escort me out again.'

The media were quick to latch on to the reports of Tom paying a bribe but he denied it. 'I was determined not to give in to blackmail,' he told reporters. 'Boy, am I glad to be out of there, it was like a cloak and dagger operation. There were armed bodyguards everywhere and even the judge was wearing a gun.'

He told the reporters that he was asked to sign a statement about the alleged assault and then the judge said 'Vamos pronto.' 'I don't speak Spanish but I knew what those words meant,' Tom said.

The reporters asked if Dai Perry had been sacked after the incident but Tom and his spokesmen said it had been a mutual agreement for Dai to finish and in no way was he sacked. 'We'll always be good friends,' Tom said. 'The Venezuelans claimed Dai was my personal bodyguard but I've never had one and never will. I'm perfectly capable of taking care of myself.' Tom kept up his macho-man image by saying Dai had merely been 'lending a general hand' on the tours. 'The most he ever had to guard was the telephone. He took care of all the calls.' Safely back in Treforest, Dai told reporters, 'There are no hard feelings. Me and Tom are more like brothers than friends. I've had enough of the flying and travelling, anyway. It's too much pressure on you.' Tom and Dai were never to work together again.

By the end of 1974 and the beginning of 1975 Tom was a singing goldmine, and his total earnings were in excess of £5m a year. For a few years now Tom and Gordon had managed to cut down their tax bill through MAM, but they both still thought it was disgusting how much the British taxman was taking from them. Tom was doing ninety per cent of his work in America and the British taxman was taking a colossal 84p in the pound. After seeing the latest British tax demands Gordon launched into a rage and decided there was only one thing for it — Tom and Engel would have to become tax exiles in America. It was no real problem. America is where they worked and spent most of their time, so why not make it easier and live there?

By 1975 Tom had joined the growing band of British tax exiles such as golfer Tony Jacklin, actress Charlotte Rampling, racing driver James Hunt, boxer Billy Walker, and novelist Frederick Forsyth.

He later said, 'It wasn't that I objected to paying British tax, but with all my earnings coming from America by then, I was paying eighty-four per cent in Britain plus a fifteen per cent holding tax in the States. Really I had no choice.' He had been prepared to give up half his income to the British taxman every year to stay in the country, but no way was he going to give more than three-quarters of it. Tom and his accountants reckoned he had paid a minimum of £7m in income tax before he was forced into exile. But Tom vowed one thing: 'I'll never give up my British passport. I like the coat of arms on the front.' For the next two years he found himself in a sort of tax limbo. Accountants were busy sorting out his affairs in America and Britain but this meant he had a limited stay in both countries. Tom couldn't go to England and at the same time he couldn't stay in America for more than six months at a time. He had to be exiled in such places as Barbados and Mexico to 'save days' on his American tax situation. He felt like a gypsy. Whenever he was in the States and found himself near the border he would leave the country to save 'tax time'. When he was in Miami he'd jump over to the Bahamas, when in New York he'd pop over to Bermuda and when in California he'd go over to Mexico.

Linda and Mark would fly out to meet him in exile. The worst time was Christmas. Tom loathed it and it showed. He said in one 'tax-exile' interview, 'I can understand people saying that they would like the same kind of problem, but I really am very homesick, it gets almost unbearable. You can keep all the sunshine and plush hotel suites. Give me some Christmas pud and a pint with the lads.' It made his blood boil that he could not even do a concert in Britain because of the tax situation. He applied for a Green Card (US residency/work permit) and bided his time.

It was while he was leading his gypsy style exile that he nearly lost his life. Vacationing in one of his favourite spots — Acapulco, Mexico — he decided to take a break from the relentless heat and go for a dip into the sea. After swimming for a while alone he got a fright when he looked back to the shore — he was more than a quarter of a mile out. The waves had carried him further than he thought and they were carrying him out even further. Tom got in a panic and began to swim back but even with all his strength he found that after five minutes he was still in the same place. The shore still remained far off in the distance. Tom's heart pounded and he began to scream for help. 'My God,' he thought, 'I'm going to die. The sea is going to become my grave.' As he struggled with the current Tom saw the faces of all the people he was close to — Linda, Mark, Freda, Tom Snr, sister Sheila, Gordon, and he was sure he would never see any of them again.

As the waves lashed over his body Tom remembered he was wearing a little cross on a chain around his neck. Swimming with one hand, he grabbed the cross and shouted, 'Oh God, please help me. Don't let me die. Please let me see my wife and son again. There's no one else to help me, only you, God.' He felt his strength gather, and put his head down, swimming like he had never done before. He swam frantically until he felt himself weakening. Suddenly a wave grabbed hold of him and began to throw him like a leaf in a storm towards the shore. The force of the wave knocked the wind out of him, he thought he would be ripped apart against the rocks. But another wave lifted Tom and hurled him through the air. A few minutes later Tom landed sprawling on the beach. It was as if God had answered his prayer.

He said afterwards, 'There's no way I could have survived that alone. It was truly a miracle.'

Tom had a yearning to sing for his British fans, and playing in a nearby country was the only solution. To please his fans he agreed to play two concerts in Paris. A British national daily newspaper arranged for hundreds of Jones fans to travel by special buses to the 3,700-seater Palais De Congress on 15 and 16 March 1976. Tom arrived in the capital of France like a king and was treated like one. He insisted on a dressing room refrigerator stocked with the best champagne and had three chauffeur-driven limousines and two motor coaches at his disposal.

For accommodation his contract stipulated three suites in the best hotel and fifteen rooms for his party. When posters were put up in Paris advertising the concerts, rampant French female fans ripped them down. Between the two concerts he sang for charity at Montreux, Lake Geneva. The screaming British and French fans welcomed Tom back to Europe with a vengeance and the receipts at the booking office made Tom more than £55,000 — far more than Shirley MacLaine or Raquel Welch had got at the same time for concerts at the Palais De Congress (When Tom and Raquel Welch appeared in each other's TV shows some time before, it was billed as 'An explosion of sheer sexual chemistry.' But to Tom it was an anti-climax. He was soon disillusioned with the hype when it took hours to record a simple duet with her on his show.)

Tom told his British fans that he was overwhelmed they had travelled over to see him and hoped that when his tax situation was sorted out he would be able to sing for them again in Britain. Sophia Loren came backstage and told him she was a big admirer. She had been thrilled that Tom performed 'The Impossible Dream' from her film The Man from La Mancha. Another visitor was Greek singer Demis Roussos. Tom and Gordon's old friend Johnny Bennett travelled over on one of the special coaches as a birthday treat. Halfway through the show Tom was to give Johnny his greatest birthday present ever when he told the packed concert hall, 'Ladies and gentlemen, all this would not have been possible if it wasn't for my mate out there, Johnny Bennett.' Sitting in the audience Johnny's pride and emotion overcame him. Later Johnny produced his diary from Tom's singing days in Pontypridd and the valleys, and they reminisced for hours. The diary was jam packed with details of the young Tom.

8. The Stud

The year 1976 was to be when Tom got the chance to act. He and Gordon had bought the rights to a film called The Gospel Singer years before but they could still not find any film company interested in financing it. The Gospel Singer was seen to have an unhealthy mixture of sex and religion. Back in the early 1970s Tom had even been linked with the James Bond part but he dismissed the rumours as nonsense. 'I could never do that. I wouldn't attempt to take Sean Connery's place,' he said.

There had even been talk of Elvis and Tom appearing in a movie but that also came to nothing. Meanwhile actress Joan Collins and her sister, writer Jackie Collins, came up with an idea that Tom play an even sexier part than James Bond. When Jackie's book The Stud was first published in 1970 they agreed that Tom would be perfect for the part. Six years later when the film of the book was due to be made, he was approached. When Tom read the script he was actually shocked. He had seen a lot of things and done a lot of things during and after his days in the valleys but this took his breath away. The dialogue was full of bad language and the script required him to leap from bed to bed like some kind of sexual superman with the morals of a bi-sexual alley cat. He said to Jackie Collins, 'There are far too many four letter words in this. Are they necessary?'

Jackie Collins replied, 'Yes. We've tried to keep it as close to the book as possible.' Tom explained, 'I don't mind swearing to emphasize something, but just to throw words in for no reason is another matter. The plot of The Stud centred around a rich woman —Joan Collins — who was married to an old Arab just for his money. There were scenes involving drugs, bi-sexuality, homosexuality and orgies. Tom was shocked at one scene where the Stud's girlfriend is with another woman and he is supposed to be with another man. It was not on; the Jones fans would never have stood for it. He was put off by another scene in the script where the so-called Stud wants to get back to London but hasn't got the money. Tom explained, 'He asks the rich lady for a ticket but she tells him, "F--- your way back." I wouldn't like my mum and dad to see that sort of film. It's just short of being pornographic.'

It was suggested that Tom had been the model for the hero of Jackie Collins's other book Lovers and Gamblers. Tom admitted that the central character had been a bit like him but objected if anyone said it was based entirely on him. 'If Jackie Collins said it was me then I wouldn't have liked it. There were things in there I would never do. And again, there were other things I would do. But it wasn't a biography. On the sleeve of the book they say it's like a mixture of Elvis Presley, Mick Jagger and myself,' Tom said.

After Tom turned down The Stud, Jackie Collins said, 'It's certainly not porny and I'm flabbergasted that Tom should have any scruples about playing the role of a super-lover.' A producer from the film company, who had watched Tom read the script, told the newspapers, 'Tom isn't what people think.

He's quite a shy guy. He was like a little boy reading the script — really embarrassed.'

Later that year Tom was given another chance to act. The film had the rather unusual name of Yuckold. Tom liked the script and accepted the part, a CIA undercover agent who was based in a seedy American ghetto. He was required to look like a bum, playing poker and shooting dice. He was to joke with friends, 'See, I've arrived, I'm a film star.' But it was not to be. Half way through shooting, finance ran out and the movie had to be abandoned. Tom asked Gordon if there was a possibility of them taking over the making of the film but Gordon advised against it, saying there were too many financial complications surrounding Yuckold. It seemed Tom's acting career was destined never to get off the ground.

By the middle of 1976 Tom and Gordon had hoped that something would be done about the high taxation in Britain. A White Paper had been published in February suggesting tax cuts but no action was taken to bring it into line with America. Tom said at the time, 'Hell, I want to come back, it hurts so badly. It breaks my heart to think I'm faced with the possibility that I'm going to have to put my house up for sale, but I'm still waiting and hoping that the British Government will see sense and bring down the rate of income tax.'

Nothing was done, so Gordon decided once and for all to move himself, Tom, Engelbert and their families to Beverly Hills, the most exclusive area of

Los Angeles, for good. Although Gilbert O'Sullivan had played successfully in America it was decided that he would be better off staying in Britain where he had a huge following. Moving from their English homes was easy enough, but Gordon had the added problem of breaking up his private zoo.

By this time he had the largest private collection of orang-utans in the world, as well as other animals on the endangered species list. Coming to live in the USA permanently posed a huge problem and it was decided that he could not keep his gorillas in cages in Beverly Hills under the cruel Californian heat. A perfect solution was found — all the animals were donated to San Diego Zoo who were grateful for such a prized collection of primates. The standing joke in the music business at the time was, 'Someone at last has made a monkey out of Gordon Mills.'

Gordon had the last laugh. It seemed his Midas touch was not only confined to the music business. One of his five gorillas fathered the first gorilla born at the zoo in twenty years. A delighted zoo spokesman, Jeff Jouet, said the baby would be named . . . Gordon.

Even in the animal kingdom Gordon Mills had left his mark. Tom had a stroke of luck when Dean Martin's house came up for sale. This commanding Victorian type brick structure stood in one of the most prestigious parts of Beverly Hills — Copa De Ora. What impressed the homesick Tom was the fact it looked something like his home in Weybridge.

It has red brick on the outside and wood panelling on the inside. After paying 1,000,000 dollars cash Tom set about making it a palace fit for a singing king. He shipped the contents of his home in Weybridge over to California. Tom said, 'Linda loved the furniture and I wanted it too. So first we found the house we thought would fit all the furniture and then shipped all the stuff, almost the entire house contents, here to America.'

Those fortunate enough to be invited to the house will see a sight that puts even Elvis's Gracelands into second place. A fountain shipped over from Italy stands grandly outside the front of the home. Inside there are fifteen rooms, nearly every one with its own private bathroom. When you walk inside you see a large winding staircase leading to a master bedroom suite and three guest bedrooms. The master bedroom is dominated by a king size four-poster brass bed.

To the right of the hallway is a dining-room furnished with a dining-table which was made in England and can seat twelve people. Beyond the dining-room is a breakfast room with a small table that seats six. That's where you'll find Tom eating most days. Through the breakfast room there is a large old fashioned kitchen with an abundance of copperware, and a red brick hearth with gas range. To the left of the entrance hall there is a large sitting-room with Victorian style furniture and deep blue velvet sofas. There is a library panelled in mahogany and adjoining the library there is a poolroom with a hi-fi. On the walls there are photos of Tom with famous celebrities. After the poolroom you walk down the hall where Tom has all his gold records hung. Discs such as 'Delilah', 'It's Not Unusual', 'What's New, Pussycat?' and 'Love Me Tonight' reminded Tom not only of the past but the fact that they are still earning money. At the end of the hall there is a large cinema room with a beamed ceiling, a stone fireplace and a bar well stocked with champagne and beer. At the back of the house there is a large swimming pool where one can laze away the hot Californian days. If Tom decides he wants some exercise to keep in trim there is a small gymnasium near the pool where he can work out in seclusion with punchbags and a rowing machine.

Tom had been in the house some time when he heard that the telephone box at Tower Street, Treforest, was to be replaced by the GPO. That telephone box was a reminder of the early days. He could remember phoning the hospital to see if Linda had had the baby and was told they had a son; 'When I was eighteen if you dialled Pontypridd 3667 the chances were you'd have got me in that box.

Pictures below and following (1) Tom with scar after car crash 1966 (2) Profile. 1980s (3) Teary Tom at Gordon's funeral .

'That call box was my first home. My first office. I courted girls from it. My family began in it (not literally mind you), and it is as much part of my life as my first gold records.'

Tom remembered the days when there would be long queues to use the box as many people in the area could not afford their own telephone. He could even remember smooching with his wife in the box when they were 'only kids'. When things started happening for him and he went to London he would phone her at a prearranged time at the phone box. On visits home at the weekends Gordon would call Tom there. 'Sometimes the news was so depressing I wished he hadn't got through.'

So when Tom heard that the box was going to be replaced with 'some new-fangled device' he wrote a personal letter to the GPO and asked if he could buy it. They agreed to part with it for £250, and it took two men and five hours to release it from its spot at Tower Street before it could be shipped over to California. Now the old button A and button B 'fourpenny' phone box stands at the side of his swimming pool. Like the old days, Tom still used it regularly. The house is by American terms a Californian palace, but when Tom was on the verge of completing its purchase Linda had her misgivings. She felt homesick for Britain and asked Tom if there was any way they could pull out of the deal.

Tom said no. Things had gone too far. So Linda was resigned to life in Beverly Hills and her homesickness was to last for years. She continued her recluse-like lifestyle and mostly stayed at home waiting for Tom to come back from long tours. At times her homesickness would become almost unbearable but Tom would tell her, 'Listen, we haven't been sent here. It's not the colonies. You can go back home to visit whenever you like. 'He noticed a strange thing after buying the house. It was never known as his house. People would say to him, 'You live in Dean Martin's old house.' It became a standing joke that the only time it would be his was when he sold it and people would say to the new owner, 'Oh yes, you bought Tom Jones's old house.'

A rich Arab did make an offer for the house after being impressed with its location and architecture. He sent a message to where Tom was playing in Las Vegas and offered him one million dollars on top of what he had paid (in effect a hundred per cent profit). But Tom was not interested. He was making enough money in Las Vegas and the last thing he wanted to do was sell the house which was his only real comfort in life, a source of relaxation after a hectic tour. On one occasion he felt it difficult to relax after being told there was an intruder in the gardens of the house. Tom's father had stopped on the stairs and seen someone running across the pool area. He shouted to

Tom whose first reaction was to rush out and see who it was. He was confronted by a youth who looked as though he was high on drugs. Tom shouted, 'What the bloody hell are you doing here?' The wild-eyed youth turned and said he thought there was a party going on. Tom said even if there was a party he would not be invited. The youth looked at Tom for a second and then said, 'I've seen you on TV, Tom. I don't mean anything.' Tom told him to get off his property straightaway. But afterwards he said he had been foolish to confront the youth. 'I guess it could have been rather bad,' he said. In Bel Air there is no need to confront such people. A superstar like Tom only has to press a button inside the house and the place would be swarming with police in a matter of seconds. Meanwhile life in the topsy-turvy world of Las Vegas showbiz continued. Tom continued to get hassle from his fans, but at other times he got hassle from fellow celebrities. One night he and his great hero Jerry Lee Lewis were having a few drinks when they began talking about managers. Tom said he never had any problems with Gordon. Jerry Lee Lewis began to run Gordon down and said he would get someone to 'sort him out'. Tom took exception to the threat and told Jerry Lee that the friend would have to sort him out first.

He was so angry he leapt up to show he meant business. Jerry Lee tried to get up but Tom pushed him back several times on to the settee. Jerry Lee Lewis's boys took exception to how their master was being treated and one of them picked up a bottle. Tom told the guy what he would do if he even tried to move towards him with the bottle.

And that was it. Both camps split up with a lot of bad temper and ill feeling between them. The next day after the effect of the alcohol and the atmosphere had worn off, Jerry Lee Lewis phoned and said, 'Tom, it's about what happened last night. Let's meet and have a friendly drink.' Tom agreed, as long as they did not discuss management and show business again. They have been friends ever since.

Perhaps it was Tom's standing in the showbiz world that enabled him to get into a near-fight with one of the music legends of his time but another music legend was to give Tom his true respect.

The name Frank Sinatra conjures up an image of exclusivity. Apart from Elvis Presley, Sinatra was the man to be held on the highest pedestal not only by fans but fellow artistes alike. Tom took along some of his family to see one of Sinatra's shows, and when Frank knew Tom was there he introduced him to the audience; there was no need for Frank Sinatra to do such a thing but over the years Tom had earned the respect of everyone in Las Vegas.

Sinatra invited him backstage and after the show Tom told his family to wait in the lounge while he went to meet Sinatra. Sinatra asked where Tom's family were. Hearing that they were waiting in the lounge of the hotel, Sinatra gave Tom a quizzical look and said, 'Well then, let's go and join them.' To the amazement of all concerned he had an area of the bar cordoned off and went out to meet Tom's family.

Sinatra and Tom would often meet after their shows finished in Las Vegas. Over a bottle of Jack Daniels whiskey, Frank Sinatra would spell out to Tom how he thought Las Vegas should be. He even suggested that they went into business together and command higher fees. But most of the talk came to nothing. When British singer Lulu appeared for the first time she got a note after the show saying 'Tom Jones would like to meet you at the bar.' She was very pleased at the request but a few minutes later she was even more overwhelmed when she got a further note saying 'Tom Jones and Frank Sinatra would like to meet you at the bar.'

Tom's old pal from his early showbiz days — Liverpool comedian Jimmy Tarbuck — received similar treatment when he visited Tom in Vegas. Tom picked up the phone and arranged for Tarbuck to have the best seats at an Elvis show and then took him backstage to meet The King. Tarbuck was amazed that Tom had such clout in Las Vegas.

Although Tom was a big noise in Vegas, Tarbuck found all the success had not gone to his head. He said, 'Tom's just the same as he ever was. Whenever I meet him in California we end up in a pub and have a few pints — he'd not changed at all.'

If Tom was receiving the highest respect from the greatest artistes in the world so too was his manager and mentor.

For years Gordon Mills had been building up a reputation in America for being a tough guy to deal with who always got the best deals for his medallion men — many so called 'big time' managers were seen to be not even in the same league when it came to negotiating contracts.

Mills was the man to be in with, and if you were lucky enough to get him to manage you then it was like being able to print your own money. One day his office phone rang and it was Larry Adler asking if he could manage him. Gordon was very pleased. He said later, 'I couldn't believe it, here was my big hero asking me if I could manage him. It was one of the greatest moments of my life.' According to Gordon, Elvis Presley himself asked if he could take up his management. Presley was not getting along too well with his manager Col. Tom Parker. It was said they rarely met and when they did, hardly ever talked, so Elvis began to look for a way out. But Gordon had to turn him down: he said that the time was not right and there were too many legal and financial complications.

By 1977 the signs were on the horizon for a change in the medallion men set-up. Engelbert had become increasingly frustrated with Gordon's style of management, telling friends that Gordon promoted Tom over him that Tom got the best deals and that Gordon's lavish lifestyle was a drain on profits. Gordon was certainly a man who spent well. He would charter a plane costing thousands of dollars rather than book a seat on a scheduled flight. He thought big and his tastes were big. At times he got bored and flew off with band leader Johnny Spence on safari spending thousands of dollars in the process. Early in the year the atmosphere between Engelbert and Gordon made things unworkable. They had a row, and Engelbert decided to leave the camp for good. The decision rocked the MAM Empire but Tom thought it had been coming for a long time.

Engelbert told the press, 'I felt trapped. My talent was being held back and I felt at last I had to do things my way.' Although Gordon had taken the then unknown Gerry Dorsey from the obscurity of small clubs to becoming a superstar, Engel was still bitter. It was as though his temper had been simmering for years as he lashed out against Gordon, Tom and Gilbert. 'I got sick of people asking me about Tom and Gilbert. Look at it this way - no man, not even Gordon Mills, could look after two entertainers like Tom and myself.' Engelbert said he was also fed up with constantly being written down as second best to Tom. He denied that there was any jealousy between Tom and himself. He pulled his weight moneywise just as much as Tom. But his complete disillusionment with Gordon showed through when he declared, 'Part of the problem was that there were many offers to me which I was never told about. I got to hear about them from third parties. 'I was not pleased, no way. Now I'm my own man. I have grown up. There was a time when I would sit back and let others do the thinking for me. But not anymore.'

And as if all that was not bad enough, the camp was shortly rocked by another sensation.

Former press aide Chris Hutchins, who had left Gordon's employment some years before, decided to dig up the dirt and reveal all through the pages of the Daily Mirror. Hutchins had been a former editor of a music newspaper and Gordon was so impressed with his style that he employed him, with his middle-class voice, mannerisms and charisma to look after his three stars. For ten years he had been their Press Officer and claimed to have witnessed every part of their private lives.

Now, in April 1977, he made a series of allegations about them, claiming among other things that Tom had had several affairs, could barely read or write, and like the other two stars was subservient to Gordon Mills. Hutchins also wrote about Engel's insecurity and Gilbert's shyness. When Mills saw the 'revelations' he exploded. It was as if Hutchins had stabbed them all in the back, and Gordon vowed publicly to break his neck if he ever caught up with him.

Meanwhile he arranged for an injunction to be served on the Daily Mirror stopping Hutchins from telling 'any more lies'.

The Daily Mirror fought the injunction in the High Court, and the three judges, Denning, Lawton and Bridge, decided that the medallion men were fair game and they allowed the articles to continue. Lawton said, 'It seems that these pop stars present one side of their profile to the public and enjoy it, but do not like it when the warts are shown on the other side. If they don't like the glare they should stay out of the limelight.' Lord Denning was equally forthright. 'If people of this kind seek publicity, which is to their advantage, it seems to me that they cannot complain if a servant or employee of theirs is persuaded that there is another side to their image which if it is in the public interest, should be known … that the image they fostered is not a true image.'

Lord Denning told Mills' barrister, Sir Peter Rawlinson QC, 'If American law were to be interpreted as you wish to interpret English law, then President Nixon might still be president. 'The revelations continued and Tom's family were said to be deeply hurt about the so-called intimate details of his life.

Hutchins was placed under guard after he received a death threat from America. The threat came in the form of a transatlantic phone call to a London showbiz journalist who was told in no uncertain terms to pass the threat on. Hutchins told the newspapers, 'I am worried. I'm taking this very seriously. I am obviously concerned about the safety of my wife and children.' Gordon Mills said in California, 'I am enraged at what Chris Hutchins has done. Now his imagination has run wild to the proportions of suspecting that I'm taking a Mafia-style contract out on him. I am going to Britain shortly but for no reason so dramatic as to threaten this man's safety. I am a businessman and I can control my rage enough to deal with him in a proper way .the law. I will see that things are put right even if it takes me ten years. 'When he flew in to Britain on 23 April it was a different story. Gone was the calm manager in California, who could 'control his rage'; in came the hard case from the Rhondda, flaming mad and vowing vengeance on Hutchins. Gordon, who was described as being in a 'tired and emotional state', told reporters at the airport that he would 'crucify' Hutchins. He said, 'Did you see that film Jesus of Nazareth? Well, what happened to

Jesus may happen to Chris Hutchins. And you can take that any way you like.

He added, shaking with anger, 'I want to see Chris Hutchins as soon as possible. I may attack him, I may take a swing at him.' When asked how he would find Hutchins, Gordon shouted, 'I know his haunts and I know the nature of the man, I can find him. 'He denied rumours that the stories had caused a rift between Tom and Linda and vowed that he would be taking further legal action. 'I come from Tonypandy where the boxing champion Tommy Farr was born. We know about action in the Rhondda Valley. 'The three medallion men were equally nonplussed at the revelations. Engel said, 'I have nothing to hide and can hold my head high.'

Gilbert said, 'I don't give a damn what Chris Hutchins says about me. He can't hurt me. I am not married and if he wants to say I have lots of girlfriends, that's all right by me. I have done nothing to be ashamed of or which could possibly upset me if it were publicized.' Gilbert compared Hutchins with Joe Haines, the ex-aide to former Prime Minister Harold Wilson. 'Joe Haines had to write about Wilson at Downing Street and now we get Chris Hutchins doing this. He has a wife and children to support and people are always interested in gossip.' It took Tom a while to hit back, but when he did he was forthright. 'I told my wife about it. Her mother also called her and warned her that bad things were being said. Linda said she never wanted to see the stories, and never did. But I felt betrayed even though the things that were written were not terrible, terrible things. He gave Humperdinck a harder time than me. 'I don't know what I would do if I saw Hutchins again. I think the best thing for me to do is not to see him. It might get me into trouble because I don't know whether I could contain myself.'

Tom said that after Hutchins had left the camp he wrote a letter saying how much he treasured Tom's friendship. Tom kept the letter but when the revelations came out he threw it away saying he'd 'strangle' Hutchins if he ever caught up with him.

Tom said they were considering suing but the damage had been done. 'What's the point? Once the words have been printed it doesn't matter if you print the following day, ' 'What you read yesterday wasn't true". You can't take back what's already been said.'

Havoc had affected the camp in the guise of Humperdinck and Hutchins, but there was more upset to come.

A few months later Tom's musical director and great friend Johnny Spence collapsed and died of a heart attack. Tom's nerves were in tatters and he was trying to cope with the shock when the next day yet another piece of bad news came through — the death of Elvis Presley.

The obese Elvis had been going through a bad time with drugs and it was said that at one stage he got into such a state he had to wear nappies to prevent him wetting the bed when he lay there stoned out of his mind. Tom had just finished a press conference in Buffalo when the news came through his road manager. Tom stopped in a hallway, leaned against a wall and felt numb. He recalled, 'It came at a bad time. For me it was a terrible thing on its own. I was slightly in shock over Johnny's death I was thinking about that at the moment somebody came up and said Elvis died. It was like, "What's happening? What's going on here?" I was shaking. It was terrible. 'Tom said of the comparisons between him and Elvis, 'Presley was aware of sex, which is part of my show also. There were other similarities through the years. We sang the same kind of songs, though he was a bit more rock and roll than me. And he was there at the start. I wasn't.' Was Tom to take the King's mantle? 'When Elvis was alive we were doing basically the same thing, but I don't think I have taken his place,' he said.

He recalled their friendship. 'When I was doing one-nighters Elvis would play a town two weeks before me and we would naturally be compared. But I liked Elvis, we got along together. He told me he had a weight problem. He was in control of most of his professional career except at the end. At the end he lost control completely. Did Tom ever see Elvis take drugs? Tom said in 1980, 'Every time he started to put weight on he'd have a problem. Towards the end he really didn't care, and let go. If they were giving him drugs I was never really aware of it. If he had drugs he never used them openly.' Tom has always hated drugs. He would tell his backing bands, 'OK, enjoy yourselves, have a good time. But if I hear of anyone taking drugs, they are out straight away.'

Over the years Tom witnessed a lot of talented people dying from drugs. Apart from Elvis, Tom knew and admired Janis Joplin and Jimi Hendrix.

He said, 'I think it is a very sad thing for anyone to get involved with drugs. But for a talent to get wasted it is a shame. I think that drugs and alcoholism are the things you have to try and keep yourself from and get in the right perspective. 'When you come from a working-class family there is not much chance of you dying from an overdose of any bloody thing because you don't have it. So when they get the money, some people indulge too much. It is one thing you have to learn that you cannot do, that the body can only take so much and that over-indulgence in anything can kill you.'

Tom's hatred of drugs stretched even to aspirins, while in the early days he was prescribed amphetamines (nicknamed 'Speed') but it was said they reached the parts he did not want them to reach. They affected his masculinity. 'I never want to experience that again,' he told Gordon. When Mark was growing up in the false and drug-ridden world of showbiz Tom was wise enough to warn his son of the danger. Hundreds of rich bored Californian youths see drugs as a way out of their boredom but Mark was instilled with the Treforest psychology. 'Have a pint by all means but no drugs. People who take drugs are weak but you've got to be a man to take hard liquor. 'Gordon, Tom and MAM may have been rocked by the events of 1977, but by 1978 they and the company were still riding high. According to the financial experts MAM performed on the stock market as though it had hit the proverbial jackpot and shares rose by a staggering twenty-two per cent during August of that year. MAM's popularity was not entirely due to the previous earnings of the medallion men but much of the credit went to the company's expansion as operators on one-armed bandits and juke boxes.

Casinos were being clobbered by extra taxes on profits but the bandits remained free of such financial drawbacks. A report by the Royal Commission on Gambling spelled out the prospect of higher profits for one-armed bandit operators. It recommended that more gambling machines be allowed in bingo halls and casinos, and in pubs token prizes be replaced with cash. During the financial year 1977 MAM under the control of accountant Bill Smith and Gordon Mills, made a staggering £837,000 out of juke boxes and gaming machines.

Jones and Humperdinck still played an important part in the company's earnings although now only half of their earnings went to MAM (although Humperdinck had left Gordon's management he was still part of MAM due to his past recordings) In the year to July 1977 the medallion men, their royalties and music publishing were producing sixty per cent of MAM's £2.3m profit. One financial expert wrote in 1978: 'MAM has now built up its other interests so much that profits should continue to grow even if Jones and the Hump decided to grow old gracefully and wave farewell to their fans.'

9. Pleasure Cove

Up until 1979 you could have fairly described Tom's aspiring acting career as 'disastrous'. The Gospel Singer had not even got off the ground. The Stud was vetoed and Yuckold was looked upon as a joke. But in 1979 an acting job once again reared its head. He was offered a part in an NBC TV movie called Pleasure Cove and gave up his only free month that year — July — to do it. Playing a smuggler, he spent days sitting about in wet clothing and said he had not felt so uncomfortable for years. It reminded him of when he worked on the building site getting his clothes soaked through with rain. When he came into show business he thought 'Great, I'll never have to wear wet clothes again'; but acting proved as great a discomfort. He said at the time, 'I'm not a frustrated actor. Nothing like that. In fact I've always looked on acting as hard work, and now I've done this I know I was right.' It baffled him how actors managed to learn so many lines. Singing was a different ball game. Songs rhymed and were easier to remember. Tom had to admit he felt better singing than acting. When he came off stage he felt great but after an acting scene he felt tired. He complained the most wearying thing was 'all the hanging about' between scenes. But acting was a must — his heroes Frank Sinatra and Elvis Presley had done well so it was natural that he should try to follow suit. He pointed out that he was not doing the movie for money — he earned more in one hour on stage than he did making the whole picture. The important thing was to get footage of himself, and it could lead to bigger and better things.

When the movie appeared on TV Tom had rather mixed reviews.

One critic wrote, 'Pleasure Cove adds up to rather tedious entertainment. Jones plays his role without much fire or variance, leaving some doubts as to any future he might have as an actor. The only time he really relaxes is during a brief disco scene when he is obviously at home.' Another critic was more favourable. 'Jones is far from terrible in his shirtless appearances. His lines are kept to a minimum and he doesn't blow them . . . the Welshman actually has some talent.' After recording Pleasure Cove Tom said: 'It was fun and easy to do although the script wasn't that good. 'But perhaps the most perceptive critic was Tom's cousin Alan Woodward. Alan visited Tom in America after Pleasure Cove had been shown in Britain and told Tom, 'If I was you I'd keep to singing! 'By the end of the 1970s the demand for Tom's singing services was greater than ever. This was partly due to the development of Atlantic City since 1978 when gambling was made legal. Within a matter of a year nine casinos were opened on the four-mile main thoroughfare and even more were to be built. Las Vegas was seen to be on the way down in the gambling popularity stakes; Atlantic City was to become the new centre for all sorts of gamblers. The big attraction of Atlantic City was the fact that within 300 miles there lived fifty million people and it was a comfortable drive from such places as New York, Philadelphia, Washington and Baltimore. Atlantic City had a different type of gambler from Las Vegas. Many of the less sophisticated gamblers came there for a short time — perhaps for only a few hours after work.

Organized buses flowed into the town and thousands converged on the orgy of fruit machines and gaming tables. Stars were seen as a must to draw the gamblers, and the casino owners were offering performers like Tom big money to make a series of appearances there.

As the big money flowed into Atlantic City the stars realized they could ask bigger fees, and as a result fees rocketed, in some cases doubled or tripled. A fee of $350, 000 was paid to Dolly Parton for one week at a casino and it sent shock waves throughout the showbiz world. Frank Sinatra was receiving $50,000 a show in 1979 but the management of the Resorts International Hotel claimed he was worth every penny, and the balance books showed it to be true. When Sinatra played at the hotel, the casino's gambling 'drop' was $6.5m larger than it had been during the same period the year before. 'We didn't fork over the kind of money we gave Sinatra because we're nice guys,' joked the hotel's vice-president H. Steve Norton. There were few stars in the Sinatra league but Tom was one of them along with Diana Ross and Engelbert who had a huge female following on the casino cabaret circuit. When Tom appeared at an Atlantic City hotel he could add millions of dollars to the previous year's gambling takings. When Diana Ross appeared at one casino she helped make a bigger 'drop' of $5m compared to the year before. When Engelbert appeared at the Resort's casino he broke all records for a July weekend. If stars such as Tom were considered the real drawing powers in the casino cities there were other stars who were dropped because they were considered not financially viable. It was said one casino, The Aladdin Hotel, made the mistake of booking Donny and Marie Osmond. The audience comprised youngsters who drank Cokes and left straight after the show. To keep in work some stars had to cut their asking prices as management complained they did not have the drawing power of other stars such as Tom. When Tom appeared he whipped the largely female audiences into a state of sexual frenzy. Before each show they would spend, spend, spend, to get charged up. And after each show they would be so turned on and elated they would spend, spend, spend again. Tom attracted the right sort of crowd.

Middle-aged, middle-class women who had terrific spending power and who brought their husbands along to the casino. During the show the husbands would also be spending at the tables as their wives got a 'Tom Jones battery charge'. The husbands had no reason to complain. They saw Tom as some kind of sex therapist who got their women worked-up and then they would take them back to the hotel and have a highly loving evening. Tom began to get letters from grateful husbands saying, 'You've done more for my married life than I can tell you. When my wife sees you she gets so charged up she's like a young woman again. 'During one show in the late 1970s a woman died after getting too worked up. She had a heart condition and had been warned to avoid too much excitement. Another fan was at every Tom Jones concert. She stayed in the best hotels and dined out at the finest restaurants. Ordinary fans were baffled by the extent of the woman's wealth, they thought she must be a millionairess or at least have a very good job. There turned out to be another explanation: the woman was arrested for embezzling more than $100,000 from the company where she worked as a book-keeper. Police investigations showed she had falsified more than 300 cheques in thirty months. So great was her embezzlement that the drain on the company's profits meant salesmen had to be laid off or take a cut in their wages, while the remaining salesmen were forced to sleep in cheaper hotels and YMCA hostels. The woman was reportedly using the company money to pay for her Tom addiction. Tom did not know her but a spokesman for him said after hearing the story, 'She got carried away. To escape the hungry claws of his female following, Tom took to wearing a cap and dark glasses when he went out but it was useless. People would come up to him and say 'Oh hello Tom, I saw your show last night and I thought you were great.'

Sometimes the fans would have competitions with each other. At one Tom Jones concert the air got so charged that one woman raced on stage, ripped off her blouse and handed it to Tom. A few seconds later another wriggled out of her hotpants and flung them in his face.

On another occasion a group of women pelted Tom with their knickers. Tom wiped his forehead with every one of them and then threw them back. He joked, 'I imagine there are a group of bedrooms that have bronzed panties with sweat stains hanging behind glass on the walls.'

Keeping thousands of women excited would take its toll on Tom. At Las Vegas he would work up so much sweat that his clothes had to be dry-cleaned after each show. But after a time the stitches began to rot and the clothes, especially the trousers, would just come apart at the seams. It was costing Tom a fortune in new clothes and he asked his tailor for advice. But the tailor replied there was nothing he could do — it was a necessary expense of the job.

Tom said in the late 1970s of his act, 'I not only suggest sex, I practically demand it. When I'm performing, I'm like a guy who has a girl cornered in a motel room with my body blocking the door. I get turned on and frankly my show is like an orgy in pantomime. On stage I'm aware of sex most of the time. There is always the sex thing when any male performer is on stage. I don't know if other singers realize it but I do and I take advantage of it.' By early 1980 Tom was the biggest regular crowd puller on the US casino cabaret circuit. Week in week out he pulled in the crowds and regularly earned himself the equivalent of a football pools win.

Tom's earning power was such that he bought a house for his mother and father and sister near to his own home in the exclusive Copa De Ora area. Tom had managed to do one thing not many stars had achieved: he kept his family together and looked after them with his huge earning power.

The only difference from the old days was that his sister Sheila had split up from her husband Ken Davies. Ken had left Sheila for another woman in Weybridge and Tom's father had taken the split badly. He vowed to kill Davies, who had worked as a handyman for Tom — if he ever saw him again. Tom was also bitter about the break up and felt the same as his father about the situation.

They were a close family and stayed loyal together through thick and thin. Tom's fame meant that he could introduce his father to all the great stars and he enjoyed seeing his dad so happy in retirement. During 1980 Tom met up with his old pal Muhammad Ali at his training camp in Pennsylvania.

Ali, preparing for his comeback fight against Larry Holmes, was glad to see Tom and asked him to get into the ring and spar with him. Tom put on a pair of boxing gloves and went into the ring. The sparring session lasted for two rounds until Ali, by accident, hit Tom on the mouth and a trickle of blood came from his lips. Tom shouted, 'I've got a thousand dollars' worth of capped teeth.' Ali hit the floor, laughing. He must have felt sorry for Tom because he drove him back to Atlantic City and even went to the show. Tom said, 'I am very honoured that Muhammad would break training to come and see me do my thing. I am also very happy that during the two rounds we sparred he didn't have murder on his mind, because in the excitement of it all I forgot to ask for a mouthpiece to protect my capped teeth . . . my front teeth almost took a count for ten on the floor.' Tom's father loved every moment of meeting the stars. Tom's relationship with him could at times be stormy but they had a great respect and love for one another and Tom Snr would say he could not have hoped for a better son. But he had increasing problems with his breathing as the dreaded black-dust disease pneumoconiosis took its toll. A miner all his life until Tom had taken him out of the pit, he was unwell for some time. Tom hired the best doctors and medical staff to look after his father but the years down the mine had taken their toll, and on 5 October 1981 he died aged seventy-two. It was as though Tom had been struck by a thunderbolt. He cried for days and was in such a bad state he cancelled a series of shows at Caesar's Palace. He even thought of giving up showbiz for good, too upset to go out on stage and face audiences anymore. He believed it would not be fair to go in front of his fans if his heart was not in it.

But Tom's mother, Freda, and Gordon encouraged him to carry on, Freda telling him that there was nothing that had made his dad happier than his beautiful singing. He was happy to have spent that last week beside his father's bed. He buried his dad close to his house in Los Angeles and he and his mother visited the grave whenever they could. Tom's spokesman at the time, Jaohn Moran said, 'Tom and his dad loved to hang out together. His dd was a lovely old rascal. Tom has always been close to his mother, but now they are closer than ever. After all if it hadn't been for his mother he might never have performed again.'

When Tom had recovered enough to talk about his father's death he said, 'My dad, paid the ultimate price that many miners do. His lungs were affected. I bet he never thought he would spend his last years, not in the valleys, but amid the palm trees of Southern California, hobnobbing with Frank Sinatra, Elvis Presley, Paul Anka, Muhammad Ali .

When Tom did pluck up the strength to go back and perform again the only thing that bugged him was the lack of recent chart successes.

His recording of the country song 'Darlin' had made some inroads in the Billboard Country charts but it had been some years since he last had his big hit. Some critics pointed the finger at Gordon saying that he had not allowed his stars to come to grips with the music of the 70s and early 80s. They said he encouraged Tom to record the sort of songs that belonged to the 60s.

The only time Tom felt insecure and questioned his popularity was with record sales. 'When I'm on stage and people are there it comes home to you all the time. You hear the applause. So they keep on reassuring you. But when you record something you have faith in and it doesn't sell you wonder. You think, "What's wrong? What am I doing wrong that it's not selling? Why do I feel that it's a good record and the people aren't buying it?" So you question yourself.' Even without big record sales and a recent chart hit Tom was still pulling them in by their thousands every week. Engelbert, who was now managed by British impresario Harold Davidson, was playing the same US cabaret circuit but the two men never talked or got together even though Engel lived not far from Tom in Los Angeles. When the critics came to comparing Tom and Engel they usually came down on Tom's side. One critic rather cruelly wrote, 'Comparing Jones with Engelbert is like comparing Benny Goodman with Artie Shaw, Elvis with Fabian, Mick Jagger with Steven Tyler. In other words Jones is an original, who despite the extremes is a major talent. Engelbert is an imitator and is hardly a substantial enough performer to be Jones's warm-up act. 'Criticism like that must have hurt Engelbert, and it was hardly unexpected that he felt bitter about living in Tom's shadow.

Tom said he could not understand Engel's attitude. He said in the early 1980s, 'Engelbert was due to play Indianapolis and I was scheduled to follow him in three months so my name was outside the theatre as a coming attraction. Engel refused to go on until they had taken my name down. Absolutely refused. I guess he feels I am a threat.' Tom denied there had ever been any feud. He said he and Engel would meet regularly socially and used to be pals. 'Now we've gone our separate ways. Separate paths. I don't have any bad feelings towards him, not one. But I know that he felt Gordon was promoting me over him and he was always my shadow. Maybe he was, maybe he wasn't, but Gordon's a businessman and he's been good for me, excellent.' he thought Gordon had been good for Engel as well but it was a matter of personal opinion. By leaving the fold, Engel had done what he thought was best for himself.

Engel said he had no fight with Tom. 'My beef was with Gordon Mills. When we first went to California Tom and I were just like brothers. We were inseparable and in each other's houses all the time.' He admitted the split had been a tough one but he praised Tom for being a 'perfectionist' and working hard at his craft.

Gordon himself was certainly feeling the brunt of his past actions. By the early 1980s his marriage to Jo Mills was in tatters and she stayed in Weybridge while he lived in America. Jo complained that Gordon had paid more attention to promoting Tom than he had to their marriage.

A costly divorce on the horizon was bad enough, but Gordon was also to have problems with the Irishman he took from nowhere, Gilbert O'Sullivan. Like Humperdinck, O'Sullivan became dissatisfied with Gordon's management and had the feeling he had been ripped-off. An older and wiser Gilbert complained that at the height of his fame in 1972 as the world's top solo artiste, Gordon had kept him on £10 a week pocket money. O'Sullivan said Gordon had duped him into signing a contract giving the manager the lion's share of his vast earnings. In 1982 O'Sullivan sued Gordon and MAM for £7 million of the £14.5 million he had earned over the years. The court case came out in O'Sullivan's favour and the judge commented that O'Sullivan had been bought 'at bargain basement prices', fleeced and exploited. Rumour had it that at one point

Gordon was so financially embarrassed Tom had
help his manager out.

10. I'm Coming Home

Throughout his career Tom kept his son Mark by his side and watched him grow up with an increasing understanding of the showbiz world By the early 1980s Mark had become not only Tom's regular companion on the road but his lighting director, and Tom admitted, 'He's the best I've ever had.' Tom was proud of his son, saying that they were so close they were just like brothers. 'Best of all, he has never found reason to rebel against me the way most sons do. And I like to think I set a good example for him. That's why he doesn't take drugs like so many other young people.' Mark has become aware of some critics on the side-lines who complained that he had never done a day's work in his life. He replied to such criticism, 'I've done what many sons of working class, close knit families do — go into the family business. I never really thought of doing anything else. Show business has been my life ever since I can remember Dad being a celebrity.' Mark would say to the criticism that he believed he performed an important part in the 'family business' and Tom liked having him around as a friend and companion. 'As long as he's happy, I'm happy,' Mark said in one interview .If anything Mark was the opposite of his father — shy with women; but by the early 1980s he had a blossoming romance with a girl called Donna Paloma. Donna was going out with Mark's best friend and living in New York. Whenever she met Mark they were always surrounded by people and since she was his friend's girlfriend nothing could develop. But Donna realized she was attracted to Mark and was falling in love with the son of a superstar. When her boyfriend asked her to move to Los Angeles she jumped at the chance. 'It sounds terrible,' she said, 'but I knew I'd be nearer to Mark.'

After two years of knowing each other he finally gathered up enough courage to confess her feelings to Mark. He told her he felt the same and both had to break the news to her boyfriend. There was no expense spared for the wedding and more than 200 guests attended the reception at a Beverly Hills hotel. As a wedding gift Tom bought them a house nearby. By June 1983 the couple had made Tom a grandfather and he was overjoyed about it. For years Tom had yearned for an addition to his family. He had confessed in 1978, 'Linda had a miscarriage after Mark and the doctor said she'll never be able to have another baby. I'd love to have more children. It's a terrible loss that we can't manage it.' With the advent of his grandson, baby Alexander, he felt that a gap had been filled in his life. He found it a bit strange to be called a grandfather. After all, how many sex symbols are called 'grandpa'? Tom, though, confessed 'Having a grandson has made me feel younger, not older.' Tom was forty-three at the time. 'Normally a grandfather would be fifty-five or sixty. At that age it would hit you more. You'd say, "I'm a grandfather, I must be getting old". But not me. I have a grandson when most people would be having a son. So I'm still young enough to enjoy it. That same year, he made a triumphant sell-out return tour of Britain. When the tickets for the two shows at Saint David's Hall, Cardiff, went on sale, queues began forming the night before and the box-office was inundated with fans demanding as many tickets as they could get to see Tom's return to South Wales after ten years. On 10 September Tom threw a lavish party for all his relatives and friends — more than 100 in total — at the Celtic Manor Hotel near Newport, Gwent. He laid on a special coach for fifty of his 'cousins'. At the hotel Tom was greeted with screaming fans and hysterical relatives wanting to get a glimpse of the man who had been away from Britain since the mid-seventies. Tom told the disc jockey at the hotel to keep on playing records. He said if he didn't people would be pestering him to sing all evening.

The party went on until the early hours of the morning and was voted a great success with 'only one punch-up' taking place. The Saint David's Hall concerts were voted an outstanding success and Tom was honoured by a civic reception headed by Lord Tonypandy at Cardiff Castle. The next day he went back to the Green, Green Grass of Home, flying into Treforest by helicopter. When he touched down at the White Tips playing fields thousands of local people gave their favourite son the loudest cheer ever heard in the valleys. Tom went back to one of his old haunts, the Wood Road Non Political Club, and the place burst at the seams with people as he walked through the bar where he and his father used to drink. It was a day showered with memories. Tom visited his birthplace at 57 Kingsland Terrace, and then 44 Laura Street. When he passed by the little corner shop in Wood Road, Mrs Vaughan, the owner, swore that Tom shouted out through the window of his limo, 'Hey missus, can I have my job back delivering papers? After his highly successful tour of Britain Tom went back on his annual gruelling tour of the USA. Year in, year out Tom undertakes such tours which take him the length and breadth of America. To show how hard he works he;

March
14. Brady Theatre, Tulsa, Oklahoma.
15 and 16. Midland Theatre, Kansas City.
17. Tarrant County Centre, Fort Worth, Texas.
18. Bayfront Auditorium, Corpus Christi, Texas.
19—22. Majestic Theatre, San Antonio, Texas.
23—24. The Music Hall, Houston, Texas.
25. The Oil Palace, Tyler, Texas.
26. Palmer Auditorium, Austin, Texas.
27. Chaparral Centre, Midland, Texas.
29. Tingley Coliseum, Albuquerque, New Mexico.

April
Civic Centre, Oklahoma City.
Convention Centre, Pine Bluff, Arkansas.
Memorial Civic Centre, Monroe, LA.
Civic Centre, Pensacola, LA.
Bouthwell Auditorium, Birmingham, Alabama.
Civic Centre, Chatanooga.
Palace Garden, Louisville.

May
1. MGM Grand Hotel, Las Vegas.
8-9. Sunrise Theatre, Sunrise.
10 Bayfront Centre, St Petersburg.

11 Orange County Civic Centre, Orlando.

12 Grenville Memorial Auditorium.

14. Wheeling Civic Centre, Wheeling.

15—19. (five nights) Valley Forge Music Fair, Devon.

23 Civic Centre, Springfield.

24 Erie Civic Centre, Erie, Penn

25 Mnt Pocono, Mt Airy, Penn.

28—June 2. Westbury Music Fair, Westbury, NY.

June 3 to July 2. on vacation.

July

3—9. Resorts Int Hotel, Atlantic City, NJ.

10. Concorde Hotel, Kiamesha Lake, NY.

11—13. South Shore Music Circus, Cohassett, MA.

14--15. Melody Tent, Hyannis, MA.

16—17. Musical Theatre, Warwick, Rhode Island.

18-20. Coliseum Theatre, Latham, NY.

26—28. Holiday Star, Merriville, Ind.

29. Five Flags Centre, Dubuque, Iowa. 31-Aug 1. Concert Hall, Washington, DC.

August

2. Auditorium, Charleston. W.Va.

3. Meadowbrook, Detroit. Mi.

4. Riverbend, Cincinnati, Ohio.

5. Wisconsin State Fair, Milwaukee, Wisconsin.

8—10. Universal Amphitheatre, Universal City, Ca.

11. Grandstand, San Luis Obispo Fair, Paso Robles, Ca.
17. Lanierland Music Park, Cummings, Ca.
18. W. Virginia State Fair, Lewisburg, WV.
20. Iowa State Fair, Des Moines, Iowa.
24. Indiana State Fair, Indianapolis, Indiana.
29. Minnesota State Fair, Saint Paul, Minn.

The shows continue all over the USA until the end of the year. This is typical of the yearly work schedule. By the end of the year more concerts have usually been arranged to add to the workload. The itinerary only includes concert dates and does not take into account the numerous appearances Tom is asked to make on TV and radio. Nor does it account for the hundreds of newspaper interviews, press conferences, and photo calls the man has to undertake

Tom's knack of 'spreading himself' all over America has meant a boom in his fan clubs. To them Tom is the king of gyrating sexuality. The Jones fans, nicknamed 'Tomcats', can be found in most American cities and towns. The name of the fan clubs and the geographical spread of them says it all.

The major fan clubs in the USA include the following:
    TOM girls of Rowlett, Texas
    The Jones Girls of Canoga Park, California
    Tom Jones Wisconsin Club of Milwaukee, Wisconsin

Tom's Soul Mates of Pittsburgh, Pennsylvania
The New Jersey Jones Girls of Kearny, New Jersey
Tom's Tennesseans, of Knoxville, Tennessee
TJ Fans Of soul, of Miami, Florida
Tom's Darlins of Anaheim, California
'Tom's Look of Love' of Chicago, Illinois
Tom Jones Goldcoast Gals, of Tampa, Florida
Tom Jones Atlanta Fan Club, Norcross, Georgia
Mr Excitement Fan Club, of N. Babylon, New York
Tom's Darlins of Kings Park, New York
TJ's Tarheels, of Newton, North Carolina
Tiger Tom Fan Club, of Valley Stream, New York
The All-American Tom Girls, of West Chester, Pennsylvania
Tom's Precious Moments, of Maspeth,
New York Mr Entertainment Fan Club,
of Flushing, New York
'Tom Terrific Fan Club' of Shelton, Connecticut
The Jones Bunch of Atlantic City, New Jersey
Me and Mr Jones of Seaford, New York
Tom Jones' Georgia Peaches of Marietta, Georgia
Tom's Bayou Belles of Baton Rouge, Louisiana
TJ's Luv Bug Fan Club of Bay Shore, New York
Tom Jones Kenner Fan Club of Kenner, Louisiana
Old Fashioned Strutters of New Orleans, Louisiana

'Bridge Across the Pond' Fan Club of Bel Air, Maryland

The Body and Soul of Tom Jones of Westbury, Connecticut.

And those are only the major clubs in the USA. It is the same story throughout Canada, New Zealand and Australia. In Britain two fan clubs exist to adore Tom: The Tom Jones Fan Club, and The Tom Jones Rhondda Boy Fan Club. Lesley Lawrie, president of the Tom Jones Rhondda Boy Fan Club, is typical of his thousands of devoted fans. In her little semi-detached house in Solihull, near Birmingham, Mrs Lawrie has turned her living room into a shrine. Large pictures of Tom Jones hang on the wall. Next to the hi-fi system lie all of Tom's recordings and on the video recorder she shows highlights daily of Tom in action from shows recorded all over the world. Like a lot of middle-aged married women, Lesley fell in love with Tom when she went to see him during the 1960s. If you ask what Tom means to her she replies, 'Everything. He helps me with the washing, he helps me with the ironing, he helps me get through life every day.' To her and thousands like her Tom is like a God; a musical and sexual guru who enters their minds every thinking moment of the day.

Tom is aware he is a sex-symbol and when on stage plays the part to the fullest extent. Most of his songs are about love and sex and Tom acts them out for his fans. He says he never takes it seriously and that way he and his fans are not embarrassed at what goes on.

Although does have many men coming to his shows, he admits he always aims his songs at the women in the audience. 'If you sing a song that is sexy you sure as hell can't sing to men. I can't sing a song and not be sexy unless I'm in a church singing a hymn. '

Even after the show fans continue to cause problems. One woman pleaded with Gordon for a job so she could be near Tom, but Gordon quite rightly refused. She burst into Tom's dressing room and pleaded with him to let her travel with him. 'You don't understand,' she shouted, 'I must be with you. I love you.' Tom told her he was happily married and such an arrangement could never be on.

When he arrived in the next town she was waiting for him. Each stop Tom made she was there. Finally Tom and Gordon found out she was offering taxi drivers personal favours if they would drive her to the next city where Tom was appearing. The police eventually had to arrest her when she began posing as Tom's wife.

In Canada they held a competition for women to meet Tom behind stage after a show. One fan sent in 1,460 applications and she did not even win. The competition attracted 18,000 entries and the promoter felt so sorry for the woman he let her join the legitimate winners to meet Tom.

In Miami a local radio station auctioned off kisses from Tom for charity. The highest bidder was one woman who offered $350 a kiss. When she arrived at the radio station she brought Tom a parcel of goodies including Russian caviar, imported cheese, a bottle of Dom Perignon and other assorted snacks. When the big moment came, however, she refused. She said she could not kiss him as she had a bad throat and did not want to give Tom an infection. A peck on the cheek is what she got for her $350.

The Tomcats are reckoned to be the most dedicated of fans and wherever Tom appeared they would arrive early to decorate his dressing room with flowers and leave an abundance of food including casseroles, cookies and cakes — all dangerously fattening to the Jones waistline. Tom has accepted for years the constant adulation of thousands of women and he will put up with almost anything. Offstage he tries to treat his fans with 'respect and dignity' but there is one thing that turns him off - women's lib. He has interpreted the women's movement as the desire of women to 'prove that they're not babies that they can think and do things on their own.'

He is all for equal pay for equal work, but 'I don't like to see women sitting in bars using bad language. I like to see men opening doors and lighting cigarettes for women.' Tom says women and men have their different roles to play and it should stay that way. 'Women when they pass the age of thirty are still full-blooded women and they like full-blooded men. That's what they get from me.'

There is no doubt that Tom's female fans are full-blooded. The fan magazines are full of erotic fantasies with Tom as the central character. A typical fantasy published in a fan club newsletter is as follows:

'You're sitting in the audience and Tom is singing. You notice Tom keeps staring at you. Each time your eyes meet, the feeling grows stronger. And you sense that tonight your wildest dreams are about to come true.

The show ends and as you are about to leave the theatre, you feel a hand on your shoulder. A voice says ' 'Please follow me". The man leads you to a waiting limo, opens the door and you find yourself face to face with Tom.

"Would you ride with me to the hotel, luv? I've seen you at so many of the shows and can no longer deny how much I want to know you better. "You enter the limo just as the light rain begins falling. Your heart is pounding wildly in your chest and your body gives an involuntary shudder. Tom asks if you have caught a chill and slips his arm around you. "Do you mind?" he asks.

'As you sit in his suite sipping the second glass of Dom Perignon, Tom is in the next room changing into something more comfortable. Soft music fills the room and the fresh clean smell of spring mixed with rain floats in the slightly opened window.

'All of a sudden you're feeling kind of heady and the reality of all that has happened sets in. Suddenly you're very unsure of yourself and your ability to handle the situation, so you reach for your jacket and go to leave. But Tom's shadow is reflected in the flicker of candlelight on the wall and in the second it takes for you to realize this, he's beside you gazing deeply into your eyes.

'You're frozen as his lips brush across your forehead; then your cheek, and then your neck. He begins to unbutton the collar of your blouse, takes a deep breath, and begins huskily singing softly to you. "You've been alone; I guess I've known about it. You gave me love and learned to live without it. Now that you've turned to go, let me beg you to stay the best way I know. Lady Lay Down beside me. Wrap all your love around me. I need you to stay, don't turn away from me now. Lady Lay Down." '

That was one fan's erotic fantasy, but the only woman in the world who has Tom as her companion in living reality is shy and retiring Linda. (written before Linda died in 2016). In the Woodward household fantasy could never really fit in. When Linda has got Tom to herself she would be more than likely to say to him, 'Hey, would you change that lightbulb?' than anything erotic. But then again, that is what married life is all about and to some extent Tom likes it. He admits his wife is a 'very clever woman' who knows him inside out. She has told Tom, 'As long as you keep coming home, as long as things are good between us when you are home, then what you do when you are away is up to you. What I don't know about I don't think about. But if anything gets back to me, you're in trouble.'

Linda leads a lifestyle the opposite to Tom's. She still rarely ventures out and stays very much in the background but is a dominant force at home. Under no circumstances will she expose herself to the spotlight of being a superstar's wife. 'I just don't see what it has got to do with me. Why should I be bothered with it? Tom's the star, not me.'

Sometimes she nags Tom to do things about the house, just like any other South Wales housewife, and Tom at times loses his rag. He has told her, 'I take more crap from you than anyone else in the world.'

If they don't argue about household chores, Tom sometimes argues with her about not going out enough. But beneath the ephemeral arguments there is still a deep rooted love between them.

In one way Linda has been the biggest victim of Tom's success. When they met and got married she expected a normal life in Pontypridd but that was not to be, and in the following years she had to put up with all the mental hassle and anguish of being a sex symbol's wife. It is debatable whether many other women could have coped with this intolerable pressure.

At times she gets very homesick and when relatives from Wales come to visit them in Beverly Hills Linda has been known to have her eyes filled with tears as a reflection of her loneliness and homesickness. But like a good wife she has stood by her man through thick and thin and the Jones's marriage is one of the longest surviving in the history of show business.

In the glamour world of kiss-and-tell Tom has to be careful what he does and who he is seen with. Tom says he probably gets away with a lot less than ordinary men do because a massive publicity machine surrounds him.

Everywhere he goes pictures are taken and gossip writers are always ready to snipe at him if they see anything out of place. Linda never goes to Tom's shows. She sees the cabaret or concert hall as his place of work which she has no part in. She only becomes involved when he arrives home after his show is over.

Sometimes Linda picks up a magazine and is hurt by the gossip surrounding Tom and some so-called 'other woman'.
'It happens all the time,' said Tom. 'I don't think that even I would have enough energy for all these ladies I am supposed to be laying! Linda's not the jealous sort but as long as I come home, that's all she worries about.'

He admits to being 'no angel' but the feelings of his wife and family have always come first. Tom has never really regretted his marriage to Linda although he is often surrounded by the most beautiful women in the world who give off signals that they are readily available. Linda married Tom when he was a nobody who had nothing. The beautiful girls may be in love with the image of the man but Linda was in love all those years ago with the reality of Tommy Woodward from Laura Street. Tom has said of his marriage, 'Linda's the one who keeps it all together.'

11. The End and a New Beginning

Tom and Gordon were in the recording studios in California during the summer of 1986 preparing for a new album when Gordon complained of stomach pains. He shrugged it off as something he had eaten, but the pain persisted and he went to see a doctor. A week later it was diagnosed as cancer. Doctors told Gordon there was nothing they could do about it as the cancer was too advanced. It was the saddest time in Tom's life since his father had died.

Over the next month he watched his friend, the genius behind his career, a man who was like a brother, deteriorate rapidly until he died at Cedars-Sinai Medical Center, Los Angeles, on Tuesday 29 July 1986. Tom was shattered and could not hide his grief. 'Gordon's death is the worst thing that's happened to me with the exception of my father's death, and Gordon helped me through that. He was more than a brother. He took me from nowhere and gave me everything. I owe him so much its incalculable. Gordon should have gone out in a 200 mile per hour crash — not this way. 'Tom looked so shattered that journalists asked him if he was considering retiring after the death of his mentor. Tom said red eyed, 'When my father died Gordon said, "You have to carry on" _so his words were in my mind. He discovered me, he influenced me, he taught me — if I stopped now I'd be letting myself and him down. Gordon's last wish was to be buried beside Tom's father in Weybridge. Tom cancelled all shows and flew over to England, and when he landed at the airport the grief could still be seen clearly on his face. At the funeral service at St Peter's Church in Hersham, Surrey, he was a pallbearer and the tears continued to gush down his face as he put Gordon to rest. Tom, Mark, and Gordon's family and friends threw roses on top of the coffin as a last gesture. Afterwards, Tom said, 'I would just like his family to know that if they ever need me, to call me and I'll be there. God bless you Gordon. "Gordon had been king of the medallion men but the other two who he had turned into superstars did not turn up at his funeral. Engelbert Humperdinck was expected but was snapped by a photographer at Heathrow Airport on the day of the funeral flying off to Los Angeles. The other Mills medallion man, Gilbert O'Sullivan, sent only a wreath saying simply, 'Deepest sympathy.' Tom revealed what Gordon's final words to him were. As he lay dying he said to Tom, 'If you ever get a pain in your stomach, go and get it checked out.' With tears flooding down his cheeks Tom said, 'He was thinking about me even then, as if I should learn by his mistakes.' The shockwave of Gordon's death was felt back in the valleys. Tom's cousin, Alan Woodward, summed up the feelings of the Woodward and Jones families. 'Tom and Gordon were more like brothers than manager and star. The years they spent together brought them very close and their relationship was one of the closest in show business. They had their ups and downs, but at the end of the day they always came to a compromise 'If it wasn't for Gordon, Tom would not be the megastar he is today.

Gordon had the driving force to put Tom on top of the entertainment world. Tom would agree that without Gordon he would probably just have been an ordinary entertainer. 'Gordon was a very forceful and dominating force as far as the business side of their relationship was concerned, and he had the charisma and charm which he could turn to their advantage. All of the show business world knew Gordon was one of the hardest negotiators for Tom's contracts all over the world. 'When I visited Tom and Gordon eighteen months ago he treated me with the greatest respect and would take me anywhere I wanted to go, although he was a very busy man. He also treated all members of our family with the same courtesy and respect, and will be sadly missed by all of us.' Some cynics suggested that Gordon's death would also be the end of Tom Jones. After all, Gordon had been the driving force all through the years, and who was there to replace him? No one could ever completely take his place, Tom realized that. As he said, 'I trusted Gordon completely. He never did anything wrong to me.' But if he was going to have a new manager he needed someone he could trust as well as Gordon. It didn't take too long to make up his mind — it had to be his son.

Mark was family, his blood, and could be trusted implicitly. Throughout the years Mark had always been by his side and knew the ins and outs of the tricky showbiz world. He had learned from Gordon and watched his cunning and shrewdness as he handled media and concert negotiators and got the best deals. Mark had served his apprenticeship under the genius of Gordon Mills and now it was time for him to come good. Under Mark's management the year of 1987 meant that Tom's career hit new heights. His single 'The Boy from Nowhere', from the musical Matador rode high into the pop charts. It was Tom's first hit in the British charts for fifteen years and it was his first appearance on the trendy pop show Top of the Pops for fourteen years. His tour of Britain was a sell out and teenagers were once again screaming at him. Major magazines and newspapers spread Tom's pictures on their front pages and TV shows clamoured for interviews. Northern Soul Clubs were said to be playing 'It's Not Unusual' and 'Delilah' — twenty years after they were hits. It was as though the Jones Boy had been lost for some years and had been rediscovered.

Tom's reply to the resurgence of hysteria was a nod of the head and the line, 'It's bloody amazing, I can't understand it. 'Meanwhile, back in America Tom enjoys life as a grandfather. Alexander has taken up the family trait of singing and one night walked on stage during a concert to join Tom. Alexander enjoyed the experience so much Tom said, 'We had to pull him off.' After one concert he and Alexander were in a car and they were listening to tapes and singing along. Alex turned round to Tom and said, 'Grandpa I want to hear you sing on one of your records.' When they got home Tom put on one of his albums. Alexander listened for a while and said, 'I liked that. It was good' Tom smiled. He had won over another fan, and perhaps the next star of the Woodward family was in his presence. It was a long way and a long time since 'The Green, Green Grass of Home', but the boy from nowhere was as pleased as punch.

EPILOGUE

As Tom hits 80 the man who discovered him and gave him his first break with an audition in a Pontypridd council house lives a quiet existence near Swansea. All those years ago bass guitarist Vernon Hopkins spotted the talent of the young Tommy Woodward and got him on stage at the Pontypridd YMCA to sing *Great Balls of Fire* with his band the Senators. His brilliant book Just Help Yourself is a chronicle of how Tom made it. Without Vernon it is debatable whether Tom would have become a star, he was an important cog in the early days and was eventually bombed out. So all these years later how does Vernon feel about it all and Tom turning 80?

I interviewed him over the phone in January 2020. He reminded me of the quote, "The past is a foreign country, they do things differently there." While Tom made millions Vernon, came out of it with virtually nothing, but he is not a bitter man. He is after all, a millionaire in memories from the day he gave the young Tommy Woodward his first break in Ponty YMCA until he became Tom |Jones superstar. "It is hard to believe it all happened to me. It's like looking at another person in another dimension. I am at peace with myself when I look back on those days with Tom. I am glad I told the story. The thing I learned was Tom is very careful with his money as was Gordon Mills, they were like two peas in a pod. I haven't seen Tom for years but sometimes I see him on the telly. I have no plans to meet up with him because he has turned 80. I often reflect on those early days and think – what was that all about? It's been a great journey and the journey is not over yet."

During the course of his 50 odd years career Tom has mixed with all the celebrities of note. Scottish singing star tells a great tale about Tom. Aged 20 she was in her Las Vegas dressing room when she was passed a note that said, "Tom Jones is in the bar waiting for you." A few minutes later another note appeared saying "Tom Jones and Frank Sinatra are in the bar waiting for you." She even turned down the offer of singing tuition from Frank Sinatra. "Tom Jones and I met him in the bar at Caesar's Palace in Las Vegas I'm 20 and suddenly I'm sitting next to Frank Sinatra. He said to me, 'Do you do any warm-up exercise for your voice, because it's very important?' Then he said, 'You should come over, I could show you how to do it.' But I was hopeless at pushing myself forward. What was I going to say? 'Give me your number, Frank. I'll be in touch?' Mind you, I was on a cloud. Frank Sinatra had kissed me on the cheek and that man was like a god in our house. But Tom was just so laid-back about it. I've known him since I was 15 and have never seen him fazed by anything. He just said, 'Nice to see Frank, wasn't it?'" Over the years Tom has also had collaborations with stars like Robbie Williams, Jools Holland and Van Morrison. He says he would love to have Robbie play him in a bio-pic.

He is often on the Jools Holland show and they have even made an album together. His old pal Van helped him record a brilliant album called Carrying a Torch which had many Morrison songs on it.

Following the passing of his wife Linda, Van's song *Sometimes we Cry* must have a poignant meaning for him.

Sometimes we know, sometimes we don't
Sometimes we give, sometimes we won't
Sometimes we're strong, sometimes we're wrong
Sometimes we cry, sometimes we cry

Not long ago Tom has been spotted on a dates with Priscilla Presley. They even went to see his lifelong hero and pal Jerry Lee Lewis perform. But he denied any romance was going on. "We've been in each other's lives for years and she is one of a bunch of people that I know in Los Angeles and we do hang out.'"

Gordon Mills was fond of telling another tale from the 70s. They got a note saying Elvis had invited them to a party in a nearby Vegas Hotel. They got in a lift to Elvis' private suit. When the doors opened Elvis was sitting in the middle of the room surrounded by some of the most beautiful women in the world. Gordon an ex-bus conductor from Tonypandy, and Tom an ex-labourer from Pontypridd gasped in amazement. Gordon nudged his pal and said, "We're playing in the first division now Tommy boy." As I am writing this in Cardiff Library two young female students sit nearby. I ask one of them does she know about Tom Jones? She replies. "Yeah it's that old guy who is a judge on The Voice." What else does she know? "Nothing really.

My mother might know but I think my granny might have a clue."

The end.

Tom at 80: his top quotes

As for the music business itself, the key things have not changed that much. It operates like any business and money still keeps things moving.

I have had some pretty wild nights! I think the media keeps a very close eye on what people are up to these days. I was out with George Clooney a few nights ago and we had a great time.

I haven't become an American! Having a house in LA is just where the house is. It's just a convenience thing living there. I carry Wales around inside me. I'd consider moving back there one day. I never really left.

I like to drink to suit my location. I love listening to new stuff, at home in LA I always have the radio on to hear what is happening.

I've always worn jewellery but for a time it went out of fashion. Like grungy and punk bands didn't wear jewellery because it was stupid.

There's plenty for me to do. There are more albums. I'll record as long as I can and as long as my voice works as well as it does now and for as long as people want to hear me.

*You can't be a sexy person unless you have
something sexy to offer. With me, it's my voice: the
way that I sing, the way I express myself when I sing.*

*I come from a coal-mining, working-class
background. My father was a coal miner.*

*I'm a lyric man - I'm always looking for meaningful
songs.*

*When I started recording, I thought I'd be able to do
all kinds of records: jazz, country, dance - and I've
always wanted to do a gospel album.*

*I thought Dean Martin always dressed very well but
then he was a good looking fella with a good
physique so he could wear anything.*

*I think the first time I ever wore a tuxedo was when I
played at the Talk of the Town in 1967, because it
was a nightclub and that was the thing to do.*

*First I got married when I was 16 so I had to do
shift-work to make ends meet.*

*I have a weakness for watches. I have to stop myself
buying more.*

*I love singing. I mean, I get out of bed and I sing. I
can't help it.
I think it's good that I had some experience of the
real world before I became successful. You know,
having to get up in the morning and going to work in
construction. Tom   When I realised I could sing for a*

living - do what I loved and be paid for it - I thought, 'This is unbelievable. Unbelievable!' And that feeling has never left me.

I've tried wearing more than one ring on one hand and it doesn't look good. It's overkill, I think. So I think a ring on either hand. Nine times out of ten I'll go for pinky rings, but not always.

I didn't have to play rugby that well, and I didn't have to play cricket that well, because I had this voice.

Music is great; it all depends on what mood you're in, what you want to listen to. If it's party time, you listen to, you know, party music, if you want to dance with somebody. But then again, if it's a slow dance, you need something slow.

I didn't like to be restricted, because when you're in a choir, you have a part to sing and you sing it. I always liked singing on my own.

I've always liked to dance - I've got a natural rhythm I don't think you can sing about certain things when you're a teen-ager or in your early 20s, because you haven't lived long enough. So I think living gives you character and that comes out in your voice.

AUTHOR Colin MacFarlane is also the writer of The Real Gorbals Story, Gorbals Diehards, No Mean Glasgow (Mainstream publishing 2007-2010) and Paolo Nutini: Coming Up Easy (Amazon 2015) The incredible rise of a Gorbals Gangster (Amazon 2020). He is also the author of the early version of this book Tom Jones: The Boy from Nowhere (WH Allen 1988)

colinmacuk@yahoo.com

Printed in Great Britain
by Amazon

72515605R10149